if you could see me now

ALSO BY MICHAEL MEWSHAW

if you could see me now

a chronicle of
identity and adoption

michael mewshaw

UNBRIDLED BOOKS

Unbridled Books
Denver, Colorado

Copyright © 2006 Michael Mewshaw

Library of Congress Cataloging-in-Publication Data
Mewshaw, Michael, 1943–
If you could see me now : a chronicle of identity and adoption / Michael Mewshaw.
p. cm.
ISBN 1-932961-20-8
1. Mewshaw, Michael, 1943—Family.   2. Mewshaw, Michael, 1943—Relations
with women.   3. Novelists, American—20th century—Biography.
4. Birthparents—Identification.   I. Title.
PS3563.E87Z46   2006
813'.54—dc22
2005033457

1   3   5   7   9   10   8   6   4   2

Book design by SH • CV

First Printing

FOR LINDA, SEAN AND MARC,
AND IN MEMORY OF MY MOTHER,
MARY HELEN MURPHY MEWSHAW DUNN
(1916 – 2005)

"The true terror . . . the true mystery of life was not that we are all going to die, but that we were all born, that we were all once little babies like this, unknowing and slowly reeling in the world, gathering it loop by loop like a ball of string. The true terror was that we once didn't exist, and then, through no fault of our own, we had to."

You Remind Me of Me, Dan Chaon

book one

One crystalline spring evening in London a long-distance call interrupted our dinner. My wife, Linda, and younger son, Marc, then sixteen, looked on as I answered the portable phone we kept near the table. Although my end of the conversation consisted mostly of monosyllables, they sensed something was wrong. They must have seen it on my face and heard the tightness in my voice. They both stopped eating and stared at me so strangely that I had to turn away from their inquiring eyes.

The call came from my sister Karen, who lives in Maryland, not far from where we grew up. My mother, now in her eighties, has a house a few blocks away from Karen, so in recent years, whenever my sister phones, I've found myself bracing for bad news. But what she had to tell me this time didn't fall neatly into the category of bad or good news, and although it caught me off guard, it had about it the sort of inevitability that attaches itself to events that you realize you've been waiting for, half in dread, half in hope, for decades.

Karen explained that she had just spoken to a woman who had called from California. "She had a very nice manner, so calm and reassuring, I assumed she was a telemarketer. She gave me her name and spelled it out for me. Then she asked me to write down her number in case we got cut off. Probably she was afraid I'd faint. That's what I felt like doing when she said, 'I have reason to believe you're my biological mother.' "

Karen's immediate reaction had been that the poor woman had the wrong number. "It was the oddest thing, though," Karen told me. "I almost wanted to say I *was* her mother. She sounded so sweet and lovely, and she had such a small child-like voice, I wanted to help her. But I told her I had two kids, a girl in college, a boy in high school, and the year she said she was born in Los Angeles, I was a senior in high school right here in Maryland."

Calmly the caller had thanked Karen and asked her to hold on to her telephone number "just in case."

"After we hung up," Karen said, "I thought of you, Mike."

Unnerved to have Linda and Marc looking on—even with my eyes averted I felt the weight of their gaze—I pushed away from the dinner table and retreated to the living room with the portable phone crackling static in my ear. Seen through the front windows of our fourth-floor apartment, the rooftops of Hampstead, all tiled in red, sloped toward downtown London. Amid the horizon's hard-edged geometry, the dome of St. Paul's and the British Telephone Tower were the only landmarks I recognized by name in this latest in the long line of my temporary adopted homes. For the past thirty-five years I have lived for the most part in Europe, yet have never settled down anywhere and have continued to feel connected to people and places halfway around the world.

"Weren't you in California in 1964?" Karen prompted me. "I remember something about a girl you followed there."

My sister and I aren't usually reticent with each other. To the contrary, we have reputations in the family for speaking our minds, sometimes too bluntly. But Karen's obliqueness was meant to spare my feelings. We had never before spoken about the months I had lived in LA.

"I hope it doesn't upset you," she said, "but I called this girl back. Her name's Amy. And I told her maybe she needed to talk to you. I didn't give her your name or number because I don't know what you want to do. But like I said, she sounds like such a sweet person."

"How did she get your name?"

"I have no idea. It must have been a mistake. Maybe this has nothing to do with us."

"Well, it certainly doesn't have anything to do with you."

"I wish you'd tell her that, Mike, because the terrible thing is, I think she's afraid that I'm her mother and you're her father."

I apologized for the distress this had caused her and promised to call Amy and correct any misapprehensions. Then I stayed on the line to Maryland a few minutes longer while Karen and I tried to piece together how Amy's search for her biological parents had led to my sister. Or, to be precise, to my half-sister. Even as kids we hadn't had the same last name, and now that Karen was married for the second time, the path to her should have been triply difficult to follow.

After I hung up I remained in the living room, looking out at the city. Lights were flickering on across the vast sprawl of London. I left them off in the apartment and sat in the dark, attempting to sort through a chaos of long-buried memories. Before we married, my wife had heard the story and accepted the situation. Now I wondered whether it was time to tell Marc. Or was that an excuse to postpone calling Amy?

I decided to contact her first, then speak to my son. Although neither conversation figured to be easy, I felt a curious sense of relief. Confession, Catholics believe, is healing. It's a chance to examine your conscience, review the past, and right old wrongs. In my case, it was also an opportunity to try to understand the past and to weigh honestly my responsibility for those rights and wrongs.

In California, where it was midmorning, Amy answered the phone at work. I had hoped to reach her at a home number. It wasn't just that I preferred to speak to her in privacy. I liked to imagine her as a mother in a domestic setting, fulfilled, secure. Yet even in an office, with colleagues nearby, she sounded friendly and relaxed, and assured me that this was a good time to talk. After a bit of preliminary throat clearing—profuse thanks for my calling, apologies for probing—she got down to her questions.

"Have you ever lived in LA?" she asked.

"Yes. A long time ago."

"In 1964? I was born on Christmas Eve that year."

"Yes, I was in California then."

"I know this is awfully sudden and may come as a shock, but I have reason to believe you're my biological father."

"An hour ago you told my half-sister you believed she was your mother."

"I'm not so sure about that."

"How sure are you about me?"

Amy didn't answer directly. Perhaps my question struck her as aggressive, and she wanted to avoid any hint of confrontation. Sounding every bit as sweet and lovely as Karen had described her, she volunteered information about herself. She told me she had been born at California Lutheran Hospital. She specified the time of her delivery and her birth weight. The Children's Home Society of California, she said, had handled her adoption, and she had grown up in the Valley. Now in her early thirties, she had had a first marriage that didn't last. It looked likely she would marry again soon, and since she hoped to have kids, she needed to learn about her family and their medical history.

"That's my primary motivation," Amy said. "I'm not looking for somebody to be my parent. I had a wonderful mother and father and a happy childhood. I don't want to barge into anybody else's life or upset you and your family. I'm not expecting a public acknowledgment of paternity. I'd just like to meet you and find my mother, but if that's not possible, I'll be satisfied with some background information and a medical history."

When I asked Amy what she looked like, she said, "I'm five feet seven and weigh a hundred and twenty-eight pounds. My hair's straight and dark brown, and my eyes are brown too."

"Tell him you resemble Sandra Bullock," someone at her end shouted.

Amy laughed. "That's on a good day and in good light. But you get the picture."

Indeed, it was a picture deeply familiar to me. Still, I hesitated to admit this or anything else. It puzzled me that she had contacted Karen. When I pressed her for an explanation, she said that new developments in adoption law had allowed her to gain limited access to data about her biological parents and the circumstances surrounding her birth. Once she received her files and what she referred to as the "nonidentifying information" from the Children's Home Society, she had hired a private investigator who turned up Karen's name.

"What about my name?" I interrupted. "Had you ever heard it before?"

She conceded that she had. During the final phase of the adoption, her adoptive mother had caught a fleeting glance of my last name on a stray document and had scribbled it down. Years later, when Amy expressed interest in finding her biological parents, her mother passed the name along. "I've known it for a long, long time," Amy said. "I've had Karen's name in my purse for over six years. It took me that long to work up the courage to call her."

"She's not your mother," I said. "I want to stress that from the start."

"But you are my father, aren't you? That part's true?"

I evaded the question and asked Amy to send me a photograph and a copy of the adoption files. Then I said I'd like to talk to her adoptive parents.

"My father's dead," Amy said. "But my mother'll speak to you. I'll call and tell her she'll be hearing from you. In the meantime, won't you please let me know something about you and my biological mother? You can't imagine how hard it is not to know anything about yourself."

Like Karen, I had a powerful urge, an almost irrational impulse, to tell Amy whatever she wanted to hear. It would be a coldhearted person who could resist helping her. Still, I held back. Hard experience had taught me caution. While as a writer I've been accused of grubbing around in people's lives, tweezing up details for my fiction or violating the privacy of friends and strangers alike for my nonfiction. I, like every author no matter how minor, have suffered intrusions and trespasses that were frightening when not downright dangerous. Nutty readers of fiction often accuse novelists of stealing their life stories and vow revenge. Sources in nonfiction sometimes believe they've been libeled and threaten legal action and physical mayhem.

In a career where the personal and professional have often overlapped, the subjects of paternity, identity and adoption have cropped up in all my books, so much so that I can no longer say whether I seek out the stories or they pursue me. Since my parents divorced when I was an infant, I suppose a psychiatrist might claim I come by my obsessions naturally. Yet there have been an amazing number of wild cards, like Amy, that have seemed to stack the deck. All during my adolescence, I lived with the fallout of a double murder committed by a friend who at the age of fifteen killed his adoptive parents. While he went to prison, his younger brother was taken in by my family. Twenty years later I wrote an account of the case and caught flack from every direction. My foster brother sued me for $6 million, and I started receiving hair-raising letters from death row inmates, renegade cops and deranged mental patients who demanded that I record their dictated memoirs.

When another grisly parricide occurred in the neighborhood—once again an adopted boy murdered his adoptive parents—police advised local newspapers that it was a copycat killing based on my book. At the time I happened to be covering a trial in Florida of a man who was convicted of killing his mother and his adopted brother. Intrigued by the case, I went on to publish a novel whose plot hinged on the suspicion that a child who was put out for adoption returns as an adult to hunt down his biological father, hell-bent on revenge, but kills the wrong man.

So, as sympathetic as I was to Amy, I thought I had good cause to proceed slowly. But she didn't agree. "Look," she said, "if there's something you're hiding, I mean if my mother's dead, you can tell me. Don't leave me guessing. Even if she's a drunk or a drug addict or a terrible person, I'd like to know, and I'd like to meet her if she's willing. I've been in a support group, ALMA—the Adoptees Liberation Movement Association—where some of my friends found out they were children born of rape or incest. No matter how bad this is, I can deal with it."

"It's not that it's bad," I said. "Just very complicated."

"You sound like you're protecting someone. Is it my birth mother or me?"

I couldn't bring myself to confess that I was protecting me. I had a family, a life, a precariously won equilibrium that I didn't care to risk.

"You know, I've seen your books," Amy said. "In the pictures on the back, especially before your hair went gray, you look like me. Or I guess I look like you. Why won't you tell me who you are?"

"I'll be glad to once I find out who you are."

From my travels in Eastern Europe, I remembered Russian dolls, each painted wooden figurine containing smaller and smaller ones. A caricature of Marx encased a miniature Lenin, then a Stalin, a Khrushchev, a Brezhnev, a Gorbachev and a Yeltsin. The symbolism suggested continuity, cause and effect, faith in a pattern and a prime pattern maker. I longed to believe in that notion—in a math or metaphysics that maps the course of life as unerringly as the trajectory of an arrow.

But in asking who I was and what I knew about her mother, Amy had uncorked a bottle that had been shelved so long I had no way of predicting whether she had released a genie or a wine that had turned to vinegar. Though bitter truth has its value, I wanted to leave Amy with more than a sour taste in her mouth. I wanted her to know that everything I might say about her mother was inseparable from the tangled skein of my own faults. And if she gleaned nothing else, I wanted her to understand that while I have regrets, I don't, I can't, I won't ever wish none of this had happened.

CHAPTER TWO

There was, though, something more immediate I wanted. Or rather didn't want, and that was to hurt my family. After I hung up, I confronted the dilemma of what to tell them. While my wife had heard a sketchy version of events, that didn't guarantee that she would continue to be agreeable if the abstract abandoned child took on flesh-and-blood reality and entered our life—particularly since this would mean that at some level her mother would enter it too.

Then there was the worry of how my sons would react. The older boy, Sean, was a junior in college in the States and wouldn't have to deal with this until later. But Marc sat at the dinner table with his mother, waiting for an explanation. Not the type to blurt out questions or betray much emotion, he possessed the practiced cool of a teenager who had had the advantage of living in England, where ironic detachment laced the air he breathed. Still, he gave me his full attention, listening with an alertness that was sometimes missing when I spoke to him about his school work or weekend curfew.

It had to have struck him as a strange, implausible tale, this story that had transpired sixteen years before his birth, when I wasn't much older than Marc was now. And it must have seemed to have occurred in a world that no longer existed. Indeed, I had a hard time believing that it had ever existed—this world where contraception when available was undependable, where abortion was illegal and the sexual ignorance of university students was on a par with that of contemporary middle-schoolers. It was a time when the Vietnam war was intensifying and the military draft dangled like the sword of Damocles over every eighteen-year-old, when communism, not terrorism, caused nightmares and an unplanned pregnancy had the capacity to ruin lives. It was a time when gasoline cost twenty-five cents a gallon, the Internet hadn't been invented, and unwed mothers were expelled from school, secretly shunted into institutions and pressured to relinquish their babies for adoption.

Marc nodded as he tried to take it in. He was a good student, an avid reader and a fellow with a fertile imagination. He appeared to have little trouble accepting that the early '60s were as different from today as . . . well, as England was from Italy, where Marc had spent the first nine years of his life, or as the States were from the rest of the world. And unless I utterly misinterpreted his reaction, he also accepted that his father had once loved another woman and that a baby given up for adoption decades ago had, against all odds and logic, found me.

No doubt Marc's attitude was influenced by Linda's. She greeted the news not just with equanimity but with something akin to joy. She had always wanted a daughter and viewed Amy as a surrogate. Then, too, the twists and turns of the story fascinated her. Like me, she couldn't fathom how Amy had tracked down Karen and reached me almost by chance.

How had she gone about her search? How long had it taken? What must she have felt all those years? And how did she feel now?

I warned Linda and Marc that there might have been a mistake. Amy might not be who she claimed to be or who she believed herself to be. She might have motives that she hadn't admitted. We couldn't be certain until she provided the information I'd asked for.

But I could tell that they didn't share my worries. Caught up in the melodrama, they couldn't see the situation except through the scrim of dozens of movies, TV specials and novels that present adoption as a genre of happy endings. The unvarying blueprint of the story as told by the entertainment industry boasts classic, even mythic, dimensions. It's a quest for identity, a journey of discovery and the resolution of a primal mystery made all the more enthralling by its potential for failure and abject misery. But the desire to recapture the past and achieve closure and emotional redemption always appears to win out.

Linda and Marc didn't need to depend on the media for examples of blissfully reunited adoptees and biological parents. They didn't have to read the ghosted memoirs of famous politicians, actors and athletes who have received a call like the one that interrupted our dinner. Here in London, the novelist Martin Amis was a friend of ours, and we knew that as a young man he had had an affair with an older married woman who had given birth to a daughter without revealing to Martin that the baby was his. She had, however, confessed to her husband, and twenty years later, after her death, the husband had told the girl the truth about her birth father.

By all accounts, the reunion of Martin and his daughter had come off without a misstep. Martin had welcomed her into his family, introducing her to his two sons by his first marriage and two daughters by his second wife. While happy to meet them, the girl had remained close to the man who had raised her, and everybody accepted it as something of a miracle that their lives had suddenly been enriched. I prayed that that was what would happen to us—a widening of the circle, a deep enrichment.

In bed that night, however, I pondered alternative scenarios. How many reunions go catastrophically wrong? Some adoptees, after being abandoned at birth, were rejected again. Others discovered too late that their birth parents were dead. But that far worse things might happen, any writer worthy of the name could easily imagine. I recalled a novel written in the 1980s by P. D. James, *Innocent Blood,* which described a young woman who tracks down her birth mother, only to discover that Mom is an infamous child murderer, now out of prison on parole. More recently, Kathryn Harrison published a memoir, *The Kiss,* about reuniting with her biological father and having an affair with him. According to psychiatrists the attraction between long-separated relatives is powerful, and sexual acting out is far from uncommon.

To prepare for problems that I feared might arrive in my life along with Amy, I decided I needed to know a lot more about adoption than I had learned from personal experience. I needed facts, statistics and scientific data. But as I would find out, such information is difficult to obtain because adoption has historically been shaped by secrecy and deceit. Unmarried pregnant women, adopted children and adoptive parents—the triad, as it has come to be known—have generally viewed confidentiality as the best recourse in a society that continues to be conflicted about premarital sex and illegitimate children. Even today, when many never-married mothers choose to raise their children alone, a stigma persists, just as it does for women who give up their babies. And although increasing numbers of people are willing to adopt children from different races, religions, cultures and countries, a premium is paid for white babies who can integrate into adoptive families without calling attention to themselves.

True, radical changes have occurred over the years. The great majority of adoptions are now "open." Birth parents and adoptive parents meet and discuss arrangements beforehand, exchanging medical and family histories, and they often maintain contact throughout a child's life. Adoption, at its best, has become inclusive, not exclusionary and guilt-ridden.

But with the growing frequency of foreign adoptions—the bulk of them originating in Russia, China, South America and other impoverished and/or overpopulated nations—children have no chance of staying in touch with their birth families or of finding them. Even in the States, the legal system places great obstacles in the path of adoptees who try to locate their birth parents. It also impedes statistical analysis and sociological studies of adoption. Instead of collecting national figures, it keeps records sealed in local courthouses around the country, and an accurate tally of adoptions would require research in every city and town in the United States.

To obtain general background, I called and left a message with the hotline at the American Adoption Congress (AAC), which advises on matters of searches and reunions. Richard Curtis, the AAC southern regional director, phoned me back promptly and offered a sympathetic ear. Adopted as an infant, he hadn't known anything about this fact until late in life, and by the time he started searching for his birth parents, they were dead. Still, he treasured the siblings and cousins he had tracked down and said that for him the truth made it all worthwhile. He decried the culture of "secrets and lies" that characterized adoptions and disputed the notion that birth mothers had received legal guarantees of confidentiality.

"You hear that all the time," Mr. Curtis said. "Mothers claim—and politicians support them—that they have legally binding agreements. But there's nothing in writing, no documentation. It's all verbal."

In his opinion, these verbal agreements were invalid and unenforceable. But resistance to opening adoption records and facilitating reunions still pervaded state legislatures, he said, where key lawmakers sometimes had a conflict of interest. Either they had adopted children of their own or they had relinquished babies and dreaded having their secret revealed.

Mr. Curtis claimed that certain adoption agencies and lawyers had a vested financial interest in maintaining the status quo. And they found common cause with conservative adoption groups that were affiliated with quasi-religious political movements. These people fought to keep adoption records confidential because of a conviction that unwed pregnant women would seek abortions if they could no longer give up their babies in secrecy. According to Mr. Curtis, there was no evidence to support this notion.

Despite his fervor about the rights of adopted children and his unquestioned belief in the benefits of reunions, I wondered out loud whether mistakes ever occurred.

"What kinds of mistakes?" Mr. Curtis asked. "You mean adoptees who don't have successful reunions?"

"No, I mean cases of mistaken identity that lead to tragedy."

Mr. Curtis swore he had never heard of any. In his experience, once adoptees gained access to their files, whether by subterfuge or with the help of a private investigator or a computer hacker, most of them found the people they were looking for. After that, 90 percent of the time, the birth mother and father welcomed contact.

Wishing me good luck with what he referred to as my "search," he recommended a book that would answer many of my questions and ease the doubts he sensed I had. Written by Adam Pertman, a former journalist for the *Boston Globe, Adoption Nation: How the Adoption Revolution Is Transforming America* was based on a series of articles that had won Pertman a Pulitzer Prize nomination. As Richard Curtis had promised, it provided an excellent grounding in the subject and supplied most of the statistics I sought. It also helped me understand that my misgivings were far from exceptional among people whose lives have been touched by adoption and whose pasts had caught up with them.

The number of these people is staggering. According to the best estimates, the United States has an adopted population of five to six million—and this doesn't include the vast number of adoptees who aren't aware of their status. When one factors in birth parents, adoptive parents and adoptive brothers and sisters, it's possible that adoption in America may directly involve tens of millions of people. In a comprehensive survey in the late 1990s, the Evans B. Donaldson Adoption Institute concluded that 60 percent of Americans—more than 150 million people!—were adopted, had given up a child for adoption, had adopted a baby or had a close friend or family member who fell into the triad. Small wonder that Adam Pertman referred to the United States as the "adoption nation."

Despite improvements in contraception, the legalization of abortion and the increased acceptance of single motherhood, there continue to be 130,000 to 150,000 adoptions annually, and there is a surplus of Americans eager to adopt. What's more, they're willing to go to almost any lengths and to pay any price. The cost of adopting a white baby in the United States now runs from $15,000 to $35,000. According to Pertman, this reflects supply and demand. With six prospective parents applying for each available baby and ready to pay whatever the market will bear, there have been ugly accusations of baby buying. Even in open adoptions, where couples cover a birth mother's prenatal care and living expenses, the generosity of the compensation sometimes suggests an unsavory fee for services. Foreign adoptions can be nearly as expensive as those in the States when one includes travel, payoffs to intermediaries and medical fees for infants who have been malnourished or poorly treated in institutions.

As Pertman cautions, the intrusion of cash into adoptions has pernicious consequences. It eliminates otherwise qualified families who can't afford the cost, and it ensures that the majority of adoptive parents are white and, at a minimum, middle class. This makes adoption appear to be a zero-sum transaction, with poor birth mothers relinquishing their babies to families of greater wealth and privilege.

Pertman, who has two adopted children himself, argues that open adoption can remedy these problems. By allowing for an ongoing relationship, it places all parties on a more equal footing and reduces the chance that the birth mother will feel exploited, then dumped. Adoption, Pertman stresses, should not be "a one-time curative event but a process that forever remains part of its participants' lives."

In an ideal world, just as birth mothers and adopted children wouldn't feel that they had been robbed of their rights, Pertman believes that birth fathers have a role to play. This notion resonated with me. Even today, birth fathers often have little say in what happens to their children. At times they don't even realize that a woman is pregnant, much less that she plans to relinquish a baby. Back in the early 1960s, there was little chance that a man might raise a child on his own or remain in contact after an adoption. In 1964, the year of Amy's birth, 80 percent of unwed mothers gave up their babies. Today, fewer than 3 percent do. Yet the involvement of birth fathers continues to be minimal, sometimes, admittedly, because men want it that way, but often because the adoption process still marginalizes them.

While it may be politically incorrect to discuss "gender differences," Pertman cites statistics that indicate substantial disparities between the sexes. Of the tens of thousands of adoptees who search for their birth parents, 80 percent are women. What's more, they are usually tracing their mothers, not their fathers.

To assist them in their searches, dozens of affinity groups have sprung up. As I had already learned, Amy had joined the Adoptees Liberation Movement Association, which had been founded around the time of her birth. ALMA, like many of its sister organizations, has pushed for two basic reforms: the right of access to original birth certificates and access to blood relatives.

Bastard Nation, as the name implies, takes a more provocative and confrontational approach. Calling on some of the same tactics as ACT-UP, the radical gay-rights organization, Bastard Nation has used everything from guerrilla theater to legal challenges and legislative campaigns to break down barriers and change the public's perception of adoption. In addition to flooding the Web with information, it inaugurated a program called Terminal Illness Emergency Search, which permits adoptees with fatal diseases to contact birth relatives who may have relevant medical data or who might donate organs.

In a country like the United States, which places a premium on mobility and where many children detach early from their families, the desire of adoptees to reconnect with their roots might seem anomalous, even slightly neurotic. Yet there's no denying the power of the emotions involved. As Pertman explains, "nearly all adoptions are initiated by women and men suffering from heartbreak and grief. For many . . . the wounds never heal." If this is true for birth parents, it is doubly so for children whose yearning is compounded by a compulsion to find out the facts no matter how painful they prove to be.

Yet I had an uneasy sense that there existed a compulsion just as powerful: the human desire to hide from a searing truth and from blood attachments that have been severed. While some adoptees will go to any expense and run any legal risk to trace their birth parents, I suspected that there are those parents whose desperation to escape the past is every bit as fierce and unrelenting. *Adoption Nation* acknowledges that there have been birth mothers who have sued to preserve their anonymity and filed civil actions against agencies and private investigators for invading their privacy. Some complain that they have been stalked by adopted children and emotionally destroyed by abandoned offspring who won't take no for an answer.

In the end, while I managed to gather the statistics I wanted, they provided little consolation. I had been intellectualizing, focusing on facts at the expense of feelings. The truth was, I realized that I was letting myself get caught up in an imbroglio that mirrored a larger, national debate about privacy and the rights of adopted children. Although willing to help Amy and to meet her if she was telling the truth, I worried how she would react when she learned her mother's identity. More than that, I worried what her mother's response might be.

CHAPTER THREE

Amanila envelope with a Los Angeles postmark reached me in London less than a week after Amy's call. Reminded of letters from college admissions offices, from publishers and judging committees for grants and fellowships, I confess to nervousness about opening it and confronting . . . what? My fate? Some ultimate acceptance or rejection?

In addition to a photograph and several pages of Xeroxed documents, Amy had enclosed a note on unlined stationery. "I hope we meet one day," she had written and signed off with "Love." Her scrupulously legible handwriting seemed that of a conscientious child. But the snapshot, a color close-up of her smiling face, showed a beautiful, vibrant woman in her early thirties. The shape of her eyes, the texture of her tanned skin, the set of her jaw with its slightly cleft chin, the lustrous dark hair, the tension of her mouth whose economical upper lip con-

trasted with the generosity of the lower one, her large bright teeth—
everything called to mind the woman I had loved.

The Xeroxed documents were in the form of a letter to Amy from
the postadoption coordinator at the Children's Home Society (CHS) of
California. Atop the first page, the agency's CHS logo had balls poised
above the C and the S and a stick figure of a child as the crossbar for the
H. Though the stick figure might have been meant to suggest a kid gam-
boling on a jungle gym, it resembled someone struggling to push iron
prison bars apart.

Dear Amy,

Thank you for your $35 subsequent payment for the additional
post adoption background information service (receipt enclosed). I have received your waiver of confidentiality which I
have placed in your permanent file.

I am sending you another waiver of confidentiality for your
adoptive mother to sign.

In reviewing your case record, the agency can provide you
with the following nonidentifying information.

As you know, you were born on December 24, 1964 at 6:36
P.M. Your weight at birth was 8 lbs. 14 oz., and you were 21" long.

Your birth mother was very attractive, bright and 21 years old at
that time. She came from a strong background with quite a complicated personality. During the time she was in California she posed
as a married woman. Her boyfriend, not the birth father, came to
California with her, expecting to marry her and to help her through
her pregnancy with you. Your birth father knew of the pregnancy
and wanted to marry your birth mother also, as well as a former
boyfriend. The decision to place you for adoption was made harder
for your birth mother because of the three proposals of marriage.

However, because of her family situation, she felt that it would be totally unacceptable and decided not to involve her family by telling them about you. Your birth mother's final decision was relinquishment, and she wanted you placed in a Protestant home with a cultural and educational background.

Your birth mother had a great deal of difficulty in arriving at her decision to give you up for adoption because she felt she would not be able to give you the things that were important and meaningful in her life. She also felt that she was being irresponsible not to take responsibility for a child she had brought into the world.

Your birth mother and her boyfriend, who posed as her brother, came into the office. They both were attractive young people and made a striking couple. He is tall and dark and she is tall, with a slender build. They were both well groomed.

Your birth mother and birth father had dated for two years and she was actually "pinned" to him. Your birth mother felt that your birth father got her pregnant with the hope of pressuring her into marrying him. His response, when he found out about the pregnancy was "now we'll be able to get married." Your birth mother did not feel this would be a sound marriage. Her family seemed to like him and she described him as a rather capable, likeable person whom she did not want to marry. Your birth father was aware that your birth mother was in California with another man.

Your birth mother's family expectations made it very difficult for her to think about settling down to a normal married existence. Your birth mother thought of her father, your grandfather, as an international consultant to the U.S. Government. He was one of the top advisors to the Korean Government for a period of years, and before that, a government advisor to the Philippines. Your grandfather was currently employed as top assistant to one of the cabinet members at the time of your birth.

During your birth mother's freshman year at college, one of her professors was grooming her to enter the Miss America Contest. She had been a runner up to Miss Maryland in that contest and was considered an attractive girl physically. She is always beautifully groomed and looks quite sophisticated. Her hair is past waist length and looks quite exotic and lovely done up in a French twist. She does not wear a great deal of makeup but has a beautiful complexion, a nice smile and a slight cleft in her chin.

Your birth father's father, your grandfather, is a retired two-star general who graduated from military school. He was 58 years old at the time of your birth. He was born in Kansas.

Your birth father was described as a large-boned, athletic, very stable, capable person who got along extremely well with everyone and was well liked. However, your birth mother felt that he had some qualms and feelings that he might not measure up to his father's expectations, and internalized all of these feelings.

The personality traits that were most unattractive to your birth mother about your birth father were that he was not a creative or spontaneous person.

Your birth mother was quite sure what she wanted to do with her life. She did plan to go to Europe with her grandmother, your great grandmother, after returning home.

This is all the known nonidentifying information in the record.

BACKGROUND INFORMATION

BIRTH MOTHER

21 when you were born

Born in Ohio

Residence at time you were born: California

Caucasian: English/Scotch/Irish/German/Swedish

5'7" tall

121 pounds

Brown hair

Brown eyes

Medium coloring

Very attractive

College graduate—English major—psychology minor

Office manager

Good health

Baptist

Single

FAMILY

Father

    57 years old

    6'2" tall

    190 pounds

    Black hair

    Brown eyes

    Very fair skin and freckles

Sometimes has hives

Good health

College graduate & graduate school in Law & CPA

Government advisor and consultant

Mother

53 years old

5'4" tall

124 pounds

Reddish brown hair

Brown eyes

Medium coloring

Allergic to fish and coffee

College and Graduate school

Judge—news field—real estate—acting

Brother

25 years old

5'11" tall

165 pounds

Black hair

Hazel/green eyes

Medium coloring

Good bone structure but light weight

In college

BIRTH FATHER

27 when you were born

Born in Texas

Caucasian: German/English

6'2" tall

180 pounds

Good build

Brown hair

Brown eyes

Medium coloring

College graduate

Advertising business

No known medical problems in the family

Good health

Protestant

Single

FAMILY

Father

    About 58 years old

    5'8" tall

    Grey hair

    Brown eyes

    Medium coloring

    Military career

Mother

    About 50 years old

    5'3" tall

    118 pounds

    Dark brown hair

    Brown eyes

    Medium coloring

> Junior College
>
> Homemaker
>
> *Sister*
>
>> 29 years old
>>
>> 5'2" tall
>>
>> Petite build
>>
>> Brown eyes
>>
>> Auburn hair
>>
>> Ivory coloring
>>
>> Junior College
>>
>> Homemaker
>>
>> Four children

I read and reread the pages, testing the meaning of individual sentences and phrases, scanning lines as though they were modern poetry that almost completely eluded interpretation. In some ways, it was a bit like reading my own obituary or thumbing through a diary kept by a coldly objective acquaintance. It bristled with double-bladed statements, some of them stingingly painful even at this remove in time.

"Your birth mother felt that your birth father got her pregnant with the hope of pressuring her into marrying him. . . . The personality traits that were most unattractive to your birth mother about your birth father were that he was not a creative or spontaneous person. . . . Her boyfriend, not the birth father, came to California with her, expecting to marry her and help her through her pregnancy. . . . The decision to place you for adoption was made harder for your birth mother because of three proposals of marriage. . . . Your birth mother was quite sure what she wanted to do with her life. She did plan to go to Europe with her grandmother, your great grandmother, after returning home."

But perhaps the most startling aspect of this supposedly "nonidentifying information" was the voluminous amount it divulged about Amy's birth mother and father and their families. The physical descriptions of her biological parents may not have been much help in her search. But the high-profile professions of Amy's grandparents—a top assistant to a U.S. cabinet member, a judge, a retired two-star general—might have suggested that all these people resided in Washington, D.C., or its suburbs.

This was an impression that could only be reinforced by the fact that the birth mother had been a runner-up to Miss Maryland. The rules of the Miss America pageant stipulate that contestants have to be residents of the state they represent. This narrowed the search to Maryland. More crucially, given the mother's age at the time of Amy's birth, an investigator could focus on a few years of the Miss Maryland pageant and zero in on a handful of runners-up.

Had the Children's Home Society revealed this inadvertently? I wondered. Or did it regard arranging reunions as its current mission?

Yet, to my amazement, with so much information at her disposal, Amy had somehow taken a false turn that had led her first to Karen and only then to me. The giveaway details about her birth mother appeared not to have influenced her at all. While I now accepted that Amy was probably the person she claimed to be, I still didn't care to admit anything until I had spoken to her adoptive mother.

CHAPTER FOUR

Now in her late sixties, remarried and residing in one of the most distant exurbs of Los Angeles, Mrs. Woodson (as I'll call her) was more than willing to answer my questions. Some adoptive mothers might be hurt that a child had decided to reconnect with her biological family, and jealous or resentful of a man reappearing after the hard work of child-rearing had been finished. But Mrs. Woodson was thoroughly positive, warm and outgoing, and took obvious pride in talking about her daughter. As she recounted how she and her first husband, George, had adopted Amy, the full story required her to tell how they had adopted their first child, a son named Jeff, who had been born four years before Amy and on the same day, Christmas Eve.

"In 1960, we did some research," Mrs. Woodson said, "and learned about the Adoption Institute, which was supposed to have the shortest waiting period for prospective parents. I remember we went to an orientation session, and people at the agency advised us of possible problems such as the adopted child might have health issues. And they emphasized that as husband and wife we had to be in this together. We both had to want it, which George and I did. So we completed the forms and expected it could be a year or more before they finished the home visits and verified our financial situation and our employment history and interviewed our families and friends, then found a baby for us. George and I had both had top-secret clearance from the National Security Agency—he used to be a cryptographer and I had been in the navy—and this process reminded me of that. They didn't ask how many times a week we had sex, but they wanted to know our religious beliefs, and they interviewed our neighbors, asking was there anything they knew that might make us unfit parents.

"I guess we passed because after only four months the Adoption Institute called to say they had a baby boy. Would we like to see it and decide whether we wanted it? I thought that was strange. It sounded so cold. Like we were comparison shopping. But I fell in love the instant I saw Jeff."

A couple of years later when she and George decided to adopt a second child, Mrs. Woodson had no preference, but George had his mind set on a daughter. A girl baby was available in 1962, but Mrs. Woodson had just had a hysterectomy and felt weak and fragile. "I just didn't think I could handle it then. It was terrible to think I might not have another chance."

By 1964, when she felt well enough to cope with a baby, the Adoption Institute had folded and its records had been transferred to the Children's Home Society of California. So the Woodsons made an application there and started the familiar ritual of interviews, home visits and background checks. This time, the agency had another source of information about the Woodsons. Jeff, now going on four, got to give his opinion of their parenting skills. Again, they must have passed, as Mrs.

Woodson put it. Within five months the Children's Home Society notified them that it had a baby girl.

"I remember they told us, 'The birth mother's a lovely woman. And
this is a beautiful girl like her mother.' Of course, that didn't matter to
me," Mrs. Woodson said. "Just as long as she was healthy and I could have
her, that's all I cared about."

I interrupted to ask Mrs. Woodson if she recalled the offices of the
Children's Home Society.

"Yes indeed," she said. "We were there a couple of times during the
application stage and a couple of more times to meet Amy. Then we
came back to pick her up."

"Could you describe the place?"

"It was a big white wooden house. It had columns and a gravel
driveway. I remember the sound of that gravel as we drove in, then
walked across the parking lot."

I remembered it too—the grinding sound of pebbles under tires,
then under the feet of a couple walking toward the house.

Mrs. Woodson went on to describe her first glimpse of Amy. "They
took us into an office. A plain room with a desk and a couple of chairs
where George and I sat. They brought Amy in. She was six weeks old
then and wearing the cutest little dress. A foster family had kept her
temporarily, and they provided us with typewritten notes about Amy's
sleeping habits and her eating schedule. It was all very clear and formal-
ized at the CHS, and the foster family had had plenty of experience.

"The first thing I noticed was that Amy had a rash on her chest. I
thought I knew what to do for that. She had dark hair, plenty of it, and
her eyes were already turning brown. I held her, then George held her,
and she never cried. There were two or three people from the agency in
the room, but I don't remember the face of anyone except Amy. I just
remember thinking, I want to get some cream on that rash."

I appreciated Mrs. Woodson's relish in recounting her memories of Amy. I understood how she felt. I found that I had surprisingly strong feelings about Amy myself and liked hearing about her early life.

"The night before we picked her up," Mrs. Woodson said, "I couldn't sleep, I was so excited. The next morning, we crunched up that driveway to CHS, and this time they took us into a beautiful paneled room with a fireplace. I don't remember whether the fire was lit or not. That's how nervous I was. Amy was in a carved antique crib. We had been told to bring clothes for her. We had to undress her and redress her so that the clothes she was wearing could go to the next adopted baby.

"On the ride home, we made a mistake. Jeff was with us, and he sat in the backseat. George drove and I sat up front holding Amy, and Jeff must have been feeling ignored. He said, 'I'm not sure we're doing the right thing, having a new baby.' I said, 'Let's give it some time.' Then when we got home, I let him hold Amy, and after that everything was fine."

Compared to the lengthy and expensive tribulation that adoption has become, this sounded blessedly short and cheap. As Ms. Woodson recalled, the total fee for Jeff's adoption amounted to $900. For Amy it was $1,200. "We were very lucky," she acknowledged, "to adopt at a time when there were lots of babies, and we could afford it. Nowadays, it would have been a hardship on a couple with our income."

The mention of money prompted a digression. Familiar with the "nonidentifying information" in the CHS file, Mrs. Woodson was sensitive to the economic and social disparity between her daughter's birth family and her adoptive family. In the majority of cases, especially these days, adopted kids come from low-income backgrounds or from deprived or even destitute foreign countries. Their adoption represents a step up, a promising new start. But Amy, whose birth parents were from wealthy families, had been raised by people of modest means until she was six. After that, her adoptive parents divorced, and she had grown up with a single mother who had to pinch pennies to provide for her two children.

"I always felt women gave up kids for financial reasons," Mrs. Woodson said. "They couldn't afford to bring them up alone. But to realize that with Amy's mom there was no good reason to put her up for adoption, that surprised me."

I pointed out that Amy's birth mother had been under family and social pressures, but Mrs. Woodson insisted, "That's not what I call a good reason. This woman needed therapy. Her image was too important to her."

I urged her to tell me more about what Amy had been like as a child.

"Oh, she was a joy to raise," Mrs. Woodson said, "and such a beautiful girl. Even when she was five or six, people stopped and stared at her. When she was still in a stroller, people absolutely fawned over her."

Mrs. Woodson laughed and admitted that while the adoption agency made every effort to match children with parents similar to them, they couldn't control chromosomes. "Amy doesn't look anything like me. I'm small-boned, petite, about 5'4", and I guess you'd say I'm zaftig. Beside me Amy always felt like a giant, but she was just tall and looked like a model.

"Even as a little girl, she was always interested in clothes. It must have been something inborn. She certainly didn't get it from me."

Mrs. Woodson recalled that Amy's adoptive grandmother had made her a dress for her second birthday. It was of green velvet, a color suitable for the Christmas season, and it had a white fur collar and a picture of a cat stitched on the pocket. Amy loved the outfit. But as a surprise her grandmother had also made a doll with brown hair like Amy's and a replica of the green velvet dress, accurate right down to the fur collar and the cat on the pocket. She presented it in a shoe box, and the instant Amy lifted the lid, she burst into tears and threw it on the floor.

It amused Mrs. Woodson to think that Amy had reacted like a clothes-conscious woman who gets jealous when someone shows up in the same dress. But it seemed to me more likely that it had scared Amy to see a miniature of herself in a box.

As Mrs. Woodson described Amy's adolescence, she emphasized her down-to-earth qualities. "She always had a lot of common sense. She was a decent student. Mostly Bs, some Cs. She wasn't really interested in going off to college, and I couldn't have afforded to pay for it. Her father didn't help much financially, and he didn't feel girls needed college. She did a couple of semesters at Pasadena Community College and worked at night at Monahan's Pub. That was a big pickup place in town, and at eighteen Amy wasn't even old enough to serve drinks. But she handled it well and was very level-headed."

It struck me that, except for her level-headedness and her lackadaisical attitude toward school, Amy's childhood resembled mine far more than it did her birth mother's. Divorced parents, money trouble, part-time jobs and lingering confusion about personal identity.

According to her adoptive mother, Amy became interested in her birth parents, particularly her biological mother, as she advanced into her teens. "'I just want to know what she looks like,'" Mrs. Woodson recalled her saying. "I told her that was normal and that I would have felt the same. Many adoptive parents feel threatened when their kids start searching for their roots. I didn't."

Mrs. Woodson encouraged both of her children to feel free to express curiosity about their birth parents. The three of them joined the Adoptees Liberty Movement Association and once went to an ALMA national convention in Las Vegas where a parent and child who had been reunited spoke of their positive experience. From local ALMA meetings, however, they gained a more realistic perspective and realized that, as Mrs. Woodson put it, "not all stories turn out prettily. But most are happy, and the birth parents say they always wondered and worried what happened to their children."

Whether reunions went poorly or well, Mrs. Woodson held the belief that adopted children have a basic right to know their origins. "The idea that third parties—doctors, lawyers, birth parents, adoption agencies—can contract away that right is appalling to me."

Still, as had been her abiding practice with Amy, she didn't push her to seek a reunion. "I didn't feel it was up to me to take control of the situation." She suggested that Amy might contact the Children's Home Society for information and left it up to her.

As our conversation drifted toward areas of deepest interest to me, I found it difficult not to hurry Mrs. Woodson along. But I let her tell the tale at her own pace, interrupting only to clarify a point or unkink the chronology.

Amy, she said, had started off her search with an advantage that few adopted children enjoy. When the Woodsons went to the courthouse to complete the adoption, there was some confusion, and as lawyers and CHS representatives and the nervous parents passed papers back and forth, an extraordinary violation of standard practice took place. Amy's original birth certificate popped up in Mrs. Woodson's hands, and for an instant, before a flustered CHS employee retrieved it, she got a glimpse of a strange name: Elaine Godot Mewsahu.

"Right away, I thought of Beckett," Mrs. Woodson told me. "It hit me that the Godot part had to be an inside joke, as in *Waiting for Godot*. But I thought Mewsahu might be the birth mom's last name."

I'm accustomed to people mangling my surname. This was by no means the most extreme misspelling. But it shocked me that it had wound up on Amy's birth certificate.

Assuming that Amy might someday need the name, Mrs. Woodson had scribbled it down and waited. The wait lasted almost twenty-two years. At last, on July 14, 1986, Amy submitted a notarized Waiver of Rights to Confidentiality to the Children's Home Society. Otherwise known as a Consent to Contact statement, this form signaled that she welcomed contact with her birth parents. If they ever submitted the same documentation, the Children's Home Society was legally free to arrange a reunion. At the same time, Amy applied for access to the "nonidentifying information" in her file.

There matters remained for several years. The CHS received no inquiries and no Consent to Contact statement from her birth parents, and Amy, regardless of how much she speculated about the past, did nothing in the present to move her search along. Mrs. Woodson, however, had read the "nonidentifying information" closely and noticed the reference to the birth mother's being a runner-up in the Miss Maryland contest. In the early 1990s, while on a business trip to Baltimore, Mrs. Woodson leafed through the telephone directory. Although she found no listings under Mewsahu, she spotted several under a tantalizingly similar name—Mewshaw—and concluded that there must have been a misprint on the original birth certificate or that in her flustered state of mind, she had copied the name wrong. Though she didn't know it, she was still thirty miles off the mark. I come from a different batch of Mewshaws who hail from the suburbs of Washington, D.C.

On her return to California, Mrs. Woodson gave the new spelling of the name to Amy and once again let her deal with it as she pleased. This time, when Amy procrastinated, one of her girlfriends seized the initiative. Pretending to be a sociology student, she called the California Lutheran Hospital and claimed she had a graduate school project that required her to pick a date at random—December 24, 1964—and track the lives of everybody born at the hospital on that day.

"Hospitals aren't supposed to reveal that information," Mrs. Woodson said. "But sometimes they do. Maybe they guess it's a child searching for her parents and take mercy. Anyway, Amy's friend learned there were a handful of babies born on Dec. 24, 1964, and just one of them was a girl—Elaine Godot Mewshaw."

At this point, Amy was galvanized to hire a private detective. She never met the man. Their conversations took place by telephone. As Mrs. Woodson and Amy both recalled it, the man was a friend or relative of Amy's first husband. In short order, he produced the name, address and telephone number of my half-sister.

Neither Amy nor her adoptive mother grasped how tenuous the link had been. As I took pains to point out to them, not a single detail from the "nonidentifying information" bears any resemblance to Karen's personal data. Blond and blue-eyed, 5'2" and four years younger than the birth mother, Karen had never participated in the Miss Maryland pageant, never lived in California and didn't have parents or a sibling who matched those described in the CHS file. What's more, since Karen and I hadn't had the same last name, and since for the past twenty-odd years she had lived under her husband's name, it was a mystery how the investigator had ever connected her to me.

As best Amy and her mother could explain it, the investigator had discovered that after three decades the records of the Miss Maryland pageant had been lost or destroyed. Still, he managed to track down a former employee who remembered that Karen had been a beauty-pageant contestant—in Washington, D.C., not Maryland—and that she was related to Michael Mewshaw. This satisfied the detective, who, without further digging, reported what he had found out.

That the search had produced the roughest draft of a very loose version of the truth, that the path to it had been strewn with lies and false documents and that it had run through people who were peripheral to the story—none of this bothered Amy. And I can't blame her. She believed she was about to locate the last piece, the key piece, in the scattered puzzle of her life. But she had no idea of the dizzying hall of mirrors she was about to enter. I knew better and feared that she might be in for a shock eerily akin to her second birthday, when the sight of a tiny replica of herself in a shoe box had provoked tears rather than gratitude.

CHAPTER FIVE

When I called to tell Amy that I had received what she had sent, I sensed her tension. Or maybe I felt so much myself that I transferred mine to her.

"My mom told me you two talked."

"Yes, we had a long, helpful conversation," I said. "She's a nice woman. You're lucky to have her as a mother."

"I know."

"She's proud of you. And I can see why. That was a lovely picture."

"Probably too flattering. But did you see anything familiar in it?"

"A lot," I said. "Your mother told me you've always wondered what your birth mother looked like. Well, you just have to look in the mirror."

Amy thanked me and added that I couldn't imagine how good that made her feel.

"You must have noticed in your file how often your birth mother's beauty is mentioned," I said. "Did it surprise you that she had three marriage proposals when she was pregnant with you?"

Amy said it sounded plausible to her. As an attractive woman, she understood what it was like to be overwhelmed by men and their attention. She had received her first marriage proposal at the age of fourteen. A friend of her brother's, a fellow in the marines, had sent her an engagement ring out of the blue and urged her to set a date. "I never even went out with him. I thought of him as a friend."

Conscious of stalling, I asked if she ever fantasized about her birth mother.

"I used to fantasize she was a bareback rider in a circus," Amy said. "Then as I got older, I wondered whether she'd be low-life trailer trash."

I had to laugh. "No, she's far from that."

"Tell me about her. Are you still in touch? Do you know where she is and how to reach her?"

"First I have something to tell you about myself."

Amy hastened to say that she hadn't meant to be rude. She wanted to hear about me too, not just her mother.

"Look, Amy, I'm sorry, but the truth is, I'm not your father."

For a moment, there was silence. Then there followed an adamant refusal to accept my word. Although she did so in her sweetest, politest manner, Amy protested that it wasn't possible. She argued that what I had said to her adoptive mother, the *way* I had said it, showed that I knew things only a father could know. "Besides, your name's on my birth certificate. How do you account for that?"

"I can't."

"It's obvious, isn't it? My birth mother gave your name as the father. Are you accusing her of lying?"

"I'm not accusing anybody of anything. She might have had reasons for doing it."

"What reason?"

"I'd just be guessing."

"It sounds to me like you're just guessing you're not my father."

"No, Amy, reread the file from the Children's Home Society. Right there on the first page, it refers to a boyfriend who came with your birth mother to California 'expecting to marry her and help her through her pregnancy.' That's me."

Amy paused before bombarding me with anguished questions. I can understand the ambivalence of an adopted child who is simultaneously anxious to reunite with her biological parents and wary about meeting the people who abandoned her. I can also appreciate the ambivalence of birth parents who both want and are afraid to be found. But the depth of my own ambivalence caught me off guard. While I felt I'd like to be honest and help Amy, I realized suddenly that I couldn't do it without humiliating myself.

"Was my mother pregnant when you started dating her?" Amy asked.

"No."

"Then how can you be sure you're not my father?"

"Believe me, there was a time when I wished nothing more than that you were my daughter. But you're not."

"You haven't said why you're so sure."

As a novelist, you're taught to value subtlety and implication, but there are times when only a blunt statement of fact will serve. "I didn't have intercourse with your mother until months after I knew she was pregnant."

"And you knew because—"

"Because she told me."

"And she told you who the father was?"

"Yeah, she told me that too."

Amy reacted not so much with incredulity as with incomprehension. "How did all this happen?"

The question admitted of no easy answer. Did she mean how did her mother get pregnant? Or how did I come to be in California with her? Amy maintained that she'd like to know both.

"She was dating another guy," I said. "They had a long-standing relationship. It went back years before I began going out with her."

"Why did you stay with her?"

Out of the volumes I might have spoken, I distilled a one-line synopsis. "I loved her."

"You loved her even after she got pregnant by another guy?"

"Yes, I was crazy about her." I chuckled and tried to lighten the mood. "Maybe I was just plain crazy."

"Why didn't you two get married?"

"I was willing. But as you must have seen in the 'nonidentifying information,' she had expectations, plans."

"Is that why she didn't marry my birth father?"

"She said she didn't love him. She said she loved me. But it must have been more complicated than that."

"What I don't understand is why she told either of you she was pregnant. Why didn't she have an abortion?"

"It was illegal back then."

"But with money and connections, she could have had one. Wouldn't you have preferred that?"

"I'm a Catholic."

"So you're against abortion in all cases?"

"I don't know about all cases. This was the only one I was involved in, and I wanted to handle it in a way that left us a chance afterward. I didn't realize until later how much I had deluded myself."

"About what?"

"There really wasn't much of a chance for us."

"But you gave me a chance," Amy said. "I'm grateful for that. I guess I've got you to thank for being born."

"I played a very small part. It was far harder on your mother. It was agonizing for her to carry you, then give you up. She's the one who deserves your gratitude."

"I'd like to have the chance to thank her personally. But I've got to say, she strikes me as one screwed-up woman."

"She was confused back then. I wouldn't call her screwed up. Even the file points out that she had definite ideas about what she wanted to do with her life."

"I'm not convinced," Amy said. "I mean, she says she loves you, but she sleeps with somebody else. She gets pregnant but won't marry either of you. Then there's the third man that offered to marry her. Where does he fit in? Why did she tell him she was pregnant?"

"I never knew about him before."

"She was full of surprises, wasn't she? Is that what attracted you to her?"

I conceded that I would have settled for fewer surprises.

"Then what was her great appeal?" Amy asked. "Tell me about my mother."

"I'd rather let her tell you about herself."

"Where is she? How can I reach her?"

I hesitated, unable to guess whether the truth would do more harm than good. Although I hadn't spoken to Amy's birth mother in over thirty years, I feared that she wouldn't welcome contact with her daughter. I feared that both of them might emerge from any meeting bruised and resentful. I also had some residual anger and hurt of my own, and I didn't care to inflict it on anybody. But as I tried to unpack my motives, I couldn't make up my mind which would hurt less—for Amy to meet her birth mother or to remain in the dark. And what would be less hurtful to the woman I used to love—being reunited with her daughter or remaining in ignorance?

Only in retrospect did it occur to me that I didn't need to make any choice. Never married to her mother and with no biological link to Amy, I was under no obligation. I could have hung up, cutting the connection. Fathers did it to their own children every day—disappeared without a backward glance. No support, no explanation. In a phrase I've never understood, they "got over it." Did that mean they forgot? Or just no longer cared?

Whatever the answer, I couldn't do that to Amy any more than I had to her mother. Call it a compulsion, call it an unhealthy curiosity, call it a persistent wish that someone would do the same for me. I'll admit to all of these.

Yet for a moment I did entertain the idea that I could simply give Amy a name and tell her to keep her eyes on the newspapers, cable television and magazine covers. Sooner or later she'd see her birth mother. In the end, though, I decided that she deserved to hear the whole story. As Mrs. Woodson put it, no third party, regardless of how well intentioned, has the right to contract away a person's life history. So I recounted it piecemeal to Amy during a dozen transatlantic calls.

book two

Apparently it is commonplace even among children from happy, intact families to entertain the fantasy that they are adopted. I never did. There were too many other explanations of why I felt like an outsider, mystified about my origins, my name and the identity of my parents.

My mother and father split up when I was an infant. During World War II, Dad was drafted, and their marriage fell apart in his absence. He claimed he received a "Dear John" letter from Mom, and although he could have fought and delayed the divorce until he was discharged, he bowed to the inevitable.

I remember none of this. I barely remember him in those days. Only one image of him comes to mind—Dad in his olive-green uniform with bright brass buttons handing me and my older brother, Pat, a silver dollar apiece. After that, he shipped out, and a sailor in dress blues showed up bearing prime cuts of beef wrapped in bloody butcher paper—a rare treat in that era of meat rationing.

Mom instructed us to call the sailor Tommy, not Mr. Dunn. Then, once she returned from six weeks in Reno with her divorce papers, she told us to call him Dad. Short and muscular, blue-eyed and slyly grinning, he would have had a matinee idol's pretty-boy looks if he'd never opened his mouth and revealed the rotten stumps of his teeth.

We continued to call our real father "Dad" to his face, but behind his back we began to refer to him as Jack, just as Mom did. Whenever we slipped up and she heard us speak of him as Dad, Mom snapped, "He's not your father. Not really. He doesn't deserve the name. Tommy's the one raising you."

When Mom proposed changing our last name to Dunn, Dad—Jack, that is—had no objections, as long as it was agreed that he would stop paying child support. Pat and I remained Mewshaws.

Given her seething contempt toward him, I wondered what had ever attracted Mom to this man she seemed to detest, this man whom I so clearly resembled. It tormented me to imagine that she might see in me the larval stage of the loathsome bug my father had become in her mind.

By Mom's account, Jack had been a gambler, a habitué of bookie joints, horse tracks and card parlors. He'd step out to buy a newspaper and stumble home days later, flat broke. Mom fulminated about squandered savings, a house repossessed, a scandal when he stole to cover his losses.

It was hard to square these dire anecdotes with the humdrum man who, after his army discharge, worked at the post office and drove a cab part-time. With his hair cropped in a brush cut and his plump face fixed in a forlorn expression, he reminded me of George Gobel, the phlegmatic '50s TV comedian whose signature catch phrase, "All-righty roo," was adopted by my father.

When, many years later, I found the nerve to ask him about his first marriage and the part that gambling had played in its failure, he curtly replied, "Whatever I did, you and Pat and your mother never wanted for anything."

I wish I had had the courage to inform my father that there were things I wanted and never had. I wanted to know him. I wanted his love and approval and his presence in my life. What I got instead—well, it wasn't without value. Early on I learned a basic premise of art—the paradoxical importance of silence in music, blank spaces on a page of poetry. While what happens to kids has inescapable consequences, what doesn't happen can have even greater impact.

Before I was out of grade school, my father and his second wife moved to Albuquerque, New Mexico, with their son and daughter. I seldom saw him again. Years passed between visits. And so he faded to a vague shape in a remote corner of my emotional map.

Yet I was stuck with his name. Although in the neighborhood I was known as Mike Dunn, at the parish school I was Michael Mewshaw, as my birth and baptismal certificates decreed. Since some of my playmates were also classmates, they wondered why my last name was different from my mother's and her two younger children's. Mom told me to tell them that Mewshaw was my maiden name. (I didn't learn until years later that only girls have maiden names.) She hated having strangers poke their noses into her business and guess that she was divorced, the great stigma for Catholics of her generation.

By my teens I had divided the world into separate compartments— those who knew me as Mewshaw and those who thought my name was Dunn—and I lived in dread that people in one compartment would blunder into the other. But as an adult I discovered that I hadn't divided the world so much as I had divided myself. I have done such a thorough job of fragmenting my identity that even now I suffer a twinge whenever I'm introduced for fear that I'll run into someone who won't recognize me until I drop my real name and say I'm Mike Dunn.

In contrast to Jack, Mom was always front and center, in my face, a monolithic figure. This didn't necessarily make her any more knowable. Like a newspaper photograph held too close to the eye, she could press so near that she dispersed into a pattern of random dots. Reaching out for her, I could never predict what I would grab. Sometimes a warm, consoling woman, sometimes a loose live wire. Her volcanic temper terrified me, and so did her devouring love. Pain—Mom's power to endure it and to dish it out—was her defining quality.

Vanishing into the hospital with no warning, she reappeared a few days later with her throat slit from ear to ear. She had had a thyroid operation and proudly displayed the scar. After the birth of a second baby with Tommy, she had a hysterectomy—a long word, she explained, that meant no more kids. "The doctor cut me open from here to here. . . ." She drew a finger from her pelvis to her navel. "And he scraped out my insides." I couldn't bear to think how much that must have hurt, yet she appeared to have no trouble dealing with it.

That was Mom. One aspect of her, at any rate. The woman could deal with anything. She coped with my father, the gambler. She coped with Tommy, who, it soon became clear, was an alcoholic. She coped with four kids of her own and ran a day-care center for a dozen other children. In middle age, she welcomed into her home a foster child whose brother had murdered their adoptive parents. Then, not finished coping, she led a twelve-year campaign to free the convicted killer.

But periodically, with no warning sign that I could discern, she mutated into another person. Into a nonperson. Her coping skills crumbled.

A blurry membrane shrouded her blank eyes. Her bones seemed to melt inside the slack envelope of her skin. For days, she didn't change out of her robe and pajamas. She sat on the living room couch, staring into space and smoking. With an ashtray balanced on her knee, she moved the cigarette to her mouth with the creepy precision of an automaton, inhaling deeply, exhaling with a sigh. When I asked what was wrong, Mom said she was dying. She asked to be laid out here in the living room in an open casket. Since she couldn't abide being shut up in a box and trapped underground, she pleaded with me to have her cremated.

No doctor was summoned, no diagnosis attempted. It never dawned on her or Tommy that a psychiatrist might help. The family held its breath and tiptoed around the catatonic woman, waiting for the mood to lift. Many years would pass before these paralyzing spells acquired a name—manic-depression—and more years elapsed before a medication was prescribed. That was long after I left home. In the meantime, my bipolar mother was as baffling to me in her manic phases as in her depressive cycles.

Ironically, I came to believe that I knew my stepfather better than my biological parents. He was a vivid character, and whether drunk or sober, he had a kind of consistency that Jack and Mom lacked. Like a lot of alcoholics, he lied about the extent of his drinking, but he was honest about why he hit the bottle. "I like how it tastes," he told me. "And I like how it makes me feel."

That it was killing him and that he might injure or kill others along the way didn't concern him. He was far from a happy drunk—when soused he was foul-mouthed, mean and occasionally violent—but his disposition when not under the influence was high-spirited and humorous. He liked to dance. He had a fine singing voice and crooned ballads in the Frank Sinatra fashion. He could whistle a merry tune and keep time jingling the change in his pocket. The life of every party, generous to a fault, he was everybody's favorite friend right up to the instant when he slipped over the edge.

With drunken blind luck, he never did kill anybody with his car, but he had some close calls. Most of them he didn't remember. In the morning, he'd notice another dent or busted headlight on his Ford and hazily realize that something must have gone wrong. On occasion, he fled an accident scene and barely made it to our driveway before passing out at the wheel. Pat and I would have to lug him into the house. In one memorable incident, the cops did catch him, and Tommy was so incoherent that he was confined to St. Elizabeth's mental hospital for observation. That rattled him, being locked up in an asylum for the insane. But once they sprung him, he went back to the booze.

At times, I hated him so much it scared me, and the only way I could control my fear was to mimic love and treat Tommy as I imagined a father would treat a son. Hate, in the end, is an extreme variation on love, and the emotional bond between us grew until we could not have been closer if we had shared the same blood.

The summer before I started the University of Maryland, I worked with Tommy at the Naval Receiving Station. He managed the laundry and dry-cleaning plant and bragged that he washed the underwear and socks of every military man in metropolitan Washington.

I unloaded trucks at the PX warehouse. The lone white in a crew of blacks, I earned $40 a week—$32 after taxes. I brought my lunch in a paper bag and ate my sandwich out on the loading dock, reading a paperback and cooling off in the catfish-scented breeze that blew in off the Anacostia River.

The black guys made merciless fun of my bookishness and razzed me about my bagged lunches. Pegging me as a sexual ignoramus, they asked if I had ever been laid. Had I even gotten within sniffing range?

My one redeeming merit in their eyes was that I knew how to play basketball. A bench-warmer at DeMatha, a famous sports factory in the D.C. area, I had dreamed of winning a full ride to college along with all the first-stringers on the team. But my best offer was a half-scholarship to Bates College in Maine. Since I didn't have the money to cover the other half, I was headed to Maryland, where I had no hope of making the team. Worse, I'd have to live at home and commute.

Tommy, who loved sports, had the tact not to mention the bleak end of my basketball career, but he liked to discuss what awaited me in college. A ninth-grade dropout, he didn't have any clue about academics, and he never asked what I intended to study. But he had firm notions about the importance of first impressions, and he counseled me that what a man wore could make or break him.

A natty dresser, now outfitted with a full set of false teeth made for him by student dentists at George Washington medical school, he explained that the laundry and dry-cleaning business had given him special insight into haberdashery. In his savvy opinion, I had some crucial choices to make before September, and I had better start thinking like a college boy.

Since he understood that I couldn't afford to revamp my wardrobe in the conventional way, he didn't suggest that we drop by a department store. Instead, after work, when he and I were alone in the building, he unlocked the laundry's lost-and-found office and let me have free rein of it. As I combed through the discarded clothing, he held forth on the collegiate look. Picking out a Norfolk coat and a Chesterfield jacket that must have languished there since the late '40s, Tommy declared that classic men's clothing never went out of style, and if I followed his tips, I'd be a big hit on campus.

The first day of freshman orientation, I took a wary glance around. Not a soul in that crowd of thousands was dressed remotely like me. The men all wore khakis, glen plaid or madras shirts and Bass Weejun loafers. I hurried home, hung my "new" school clothes in the closet and never put them on again. Instead, I wore blue jeans and work shirts, some of them also hand-me-downs from the lost and found. While these weren't as ridiculous as the museum pieces Tommy had recommended, I still looked and felt out of place.

In the early 1960s, the University of Maryland had strict tribal mores and a social hierarchy as elaborate as the Indian caste system. According to a cruelly accurate article in the student newspaper, the *Diamond-back,* sorority girls and fraternity boys occupied the loftiest rung of the ladder. Common dorm dwellers fell in the middle. And commuters were consigned to the lower depths. That was my status, and I could no more escape it than an Untouchable could pass as a Brahmin.

From my assigned parking slot, I had to hike a mile to classes. The size of a small city, the university was America in miniature, which naturally, in that day, meant there was no public transportation to connect distant corners of the campus or to link the university to surrounding communities.

I had barely had time to lament my lot as a commuter before things got worse. Since my older brother was in the air force and didn't need a car, he let me drive his. But in October, a speeding driver T-boned me at an intersection, totaling Pat's Plymouth. Once the insurance company paid up, Pat decided not to buy another car, and I found myself downgraded into a category so obscure that it didn't even register on most students' consciousness: I became a commuter who hitchhiked.

Our house was four miles from the university, too far to walk on a regular basis. In dry weather, the trip wasn't too bad. On rainy days, I wrapped my books in newspapers and tucked them under my coat. While waiting for somebody to take mercy and give me a lift, I must have looked like a pregnant woman stranded on the roadside. In class I sat beside a radiator to dry my shoes and socks.

At the end of each day, I skulked past the intramural fields, where the university marching band practiced, then past Albrecht's drugstore, where the Greeks gathered for Cokes and grilled-cheese sandwiches, and down sorority row, where frat boys often serenaded girls who had just been pinned. I didn't stick out my thumb until I reached the railroad tracks. Although misery is supposed to love company, I desperately didn't want to be recognized by anybody from my classes. In fact, it was rare that a student stopped for me. Mostly I rode with guys in pickup trucks or traveling salesmen who said, "Bet a big boy like you gets a lot of pussy over at the university."

Had I had a sense of humor or a better grasp of literary history, I might have viewed myself as smack in the middle of the American mainstream. Fitzgerald hopping a train east from Minnesota to Princeton, Thomas Wolfe traveling north from the Carolinas to Harvard, Alfred Kazin catching the subway from Brooklyn to Manhattan. After all, how did my daily jaunt over the back roads of Prince Georges County differ from their journeys across the nation's cultural divide?

Rather than count the ways, I'll simply say that I didn't feel like an intellectual pilgrim back then. I felt like a jerk learning to be ashamed not of my ignorance but of my clothes, my empty pockets and my family.

Great droves of commuters congregated each day at the Student Union. A vast, white-columned building, it was a full-service facility featuring dining rooms, snack bars, ballrooms, pool tables, a movie theater and the campus radio station. Subsiding into its seductive embrace, some commuters found it difficult to leave the place. They punched in every morning, punctual as hourly wage earners, slugged back cups of coffee, smoked, shot the bull, caught midafternoon naps in the lounges, then either headed for home or stayed on for club meetings, talent shows and sock hops. While it's possible that some of them actually studied there, they would have had a hard time concentrating, and the most common refrain was: "Looks like I've missed botany lab again."

In a memorable incident, one well-known character, a kind of unofficial mayor of the Student Union, killed himself shortly before he was scheduled to graduate. His devastated family and bereft fiancée swore that they had no idea why he had done it. An honor student in engineering, never for a minute depressed or, God forbid, suicidal, he had had everything to live for.

Reporters from the *Washington Post,* in the course of fact checking, discovered discrepancies in the story. The fellow wasn't an honors engineering major after all, nor was he about to graduate. In fact, for the past three years he hadn't registered for courses. Having flunked out at the end of his freshman year, he had never reenrolled. Instead he continued to maintain perfect attendance at the Student Union, regaling a captive audience with tall tales of his academic progress. There he met and wooed his now shattered girlfriend, compiled a fictitious résumé, mailed it out to prospective employers and interviewed with major corporations. Then, when it became clear that he was about to be unmasked, he decided to get on with his imaginary life by putting a bullet in his brain.

Terrified by this cautionary tale, which struck me as a perfect symbol of the huge university's climate of personal disintegration, I stayed away from the Student Union. I ate lunch in the bowels of the Arts and Sciences building, wolfing down a cheeseburger coughed up from a vending machine. Then I retreated to McKeldin Library, to a secluded carrel deep in the stacks. This was as close as I came to having a room of my own, far out of range of the chaos at home. A grade-obsessed grind, I reviewed my class notes, memorized French vocabulary flash cards, crammed for exams and committed my first halting attempts at writing.

These embryonic efforts read less like fiction than travelogues or instructional pamphlets. I soon realized that I needed to infuse my prose with poetry, my landscapes with living characters and my stories with coherent plots. But these were the very elements missing from my life—plot, people, poetry. Since I was entranced by Lawrence Durrell—what a pungent bouillabaisse he spooned up!—I thought the answer might be to move to Alexandria—Egypt, not the Virginia suburb—fall for a sexually inscrutable woman like Justine and write about her.

What sustained me in those days was the belief that better things—a literary career, a life of travel and adventure and, of course, love—lay in the not-too-distant future. Irredeemably romantic, an avid reader of novels, which I regarded as self-help manuals, I had formulated nothing so concrete as a plan. But I had my dreams.

By my junior year I had published several short stories in the *Calvert Review,* the campus literary magazine, and was in the running to become its editor the following year. Self-selected artistes, those of us at the magazine managed to remain superficially collegial despite our competitiveness. Secretly, each of us was convinced that he alone had talent and would make it.

I say "he," well aware of not adding "or she." In that era, even in the enlightened precincts of a literary review, "or she" was apt to be a secretary or, at best, an art editor. Creativity, like much else, was deemed to be a masculine prerogative.

But one coed, notable for her beauty and her improbable background, did publish in the *Calvert Review,* and her story, set in postwar

Korea, was as delicately crafted as an oriental fan. Compared to the earnest imitations of Hemingway and Faulkner the rest of us wrote, her work had the feel of something carefully observed and freshly conceived.

The girl—I'll call her Adrienne Daly—seemed to me every bit as exotic as her story. Her curriculum vitae might suggest a typical female college celebrity, circa 1964—sorority sweetheart, lead actress in the spring play, president of this, chairwoman of that, runner-up in the Miss Maryland pageant—but Adrienne was different. She didn't look like a college coed, and she didn't dress like one. Tall and raven-tressed, she was glamorous, sophisticated, not pert and cute. She didn't wear the then-popular kilts or culottes, plaid skirts and fluffy angora sweaters. She favored conservatively cut suits and silk blouses in muted colors, and while other girls wore saddle shoes or flats, she wore high heels and wound a foulard scarf around her lovely neck. Pinning her long hair up in a chignon, she had the aplomb of a movie star, someone always on stage. Indeed, drama ran a close second to politics as her preferred extracurricular activity. Writing for her was a sideline.

A salacious rumor had it that she was the mistress of a professor who was grooming her for the next big step. This slight smudge on her reputation added to her allure and, in my mind, compensated for the fact that she was president of the Young Republicans. Not so much politically apathetic as antagonistic to all authority, I regarded any indication of conventionality in Adrienne Daly as an aberration, further evidence of her resistance to easy categorization.

To the amazement of everyone at the *Calvert Review,* Adrienne agreed to go out with a friend of mine. Less confident and nimble-footed, I had hesitated and lost my chance. But my friend, Tom, didn't have a driver's license, and he asked me to double-date, assuming that I could borrow my foster brother's car. The four of us went to an Ingmar Bergman film, then afterward, in a bold, self-congratulatory move for white kids, we stopped at the Bohemian Caverns, a black jazz club close to Howard University. Of the girl I brought along that night I have, shamefully, not a single memory. Adrienne Daly captured my complete attention.

I noticed reddish glints in her black hair and greenish flecks in her brown eyes. One eye wandered slightly when she was tired, and I thought this was as sexy as a sly wink. She wore a scent that I later learned was Estée Lauder, and later still learned with her help to pronounce correctly. She smoked, a common vice at the time, but she had a way with cigarettes that was new to me. Rather than light them herself, she passed the closest man a book of matches, then cupped his hand and guided the flame toward her luscious red mouth. Whenever Tom was slow on the uptake, I did the honors, delighting in the touch of her fingertips, intoxicated by her perfume as I leaned close.

Adrienne spoke with precision—no giggling and gushing. This impressed me, though I can't recall what she said. I was too preoccupied by a fascinating flaw in her perfection; she had a gap between her front teeth.

By the end of the evening, Tom had abandoned the field to me. Or perhaps his withdrawal was dread anticipation of the moment of reckoning. When the bill arrived, he confessed that he was out of money. I didn't have enough to cover the check alone, and naturally, having been ignored all night, my date didn't offer to dip into her purse. But Adrienne slipped me a fistful of cash, and this gesture, done with grace, endeared her to me all the more.

Back in College Park, I dropped my date at her dorm, and when I came back to the car, Adrienne was up front in the passenger's seat and Tom was outside leaning against the fender. He said that Adrienne realized she wouldn't make the curfew at her sorority house and had signed out overnight. She needed a ride to her family's home.

"Let's go," I said. It didn't matter to me if she lived in New York or New Delhi; I welcomed spending more time with her.

"She lives in Bethesda," Tom said. "I'm tired. I don't feel like going there and back. Do me a favor. You take her."

Jubilant, I told Tom, "Sure," piled into the car and commenced talking nonstop. I can't blame alcohol—I didn't drink in those days. I was simply dizzied by Adrienne Daly.

Passably glib in other situations, I had never had much of a line with ladies. Not until now. I told her that because of her beauty, I'd bet men failed to appreciate her intelligence, and since she was so articulate, they might not notice what a patient listener she was. I said that while I often saw her in crowds, she had a striking quality of solitude, almost loneliness. Though tall, she conveyed an impression of adorable petiteness. Despite her dark hair, she radiated brightness. Slim as she was, she looked voluptuous.

Tiptoeing onto trickier ground, I claimed that I had read in an anthropology book that among certain tribes females with a space between their front teeth were regarded as having a passionate nature.

"I guess you could call me high-strung," she conceded. "But the problem is, I sleep with a retainer."

The word "retainer" conjured in my addled brain a faithful family servant. Lost in turmoil, it took me a moment to realize she was talking about a metal brace that she wore in her mouth at night. Relieved, I picked up the thread and said that although on the surface she appeared happy, I sensed a kind of sad yearning at her core.

"How do you know all this?" She slid around in the seat, leaning against the door to look at me as I drove.

"I know because you and I are a lot alike."

"That's silly. You don't have a clue who I am."

I should have heeded what she said. I didn't know her. It was doubtful I ever would. But I wasn't listening to Adrienne. I was too busy yakking, inventing the woman I wanted her to be and imagining myself as the man she might love.

At her parents' house, I remembered the money she had given me and promised to repay it. She told me not to bother. She needed a ride back to campus the next evening, and if I'd drive her, we'd call the debt even. I agreed—as long as she'd let me take her to another movie. We sealed the deal with a handshake. Then she sat tight while I scooted around and opened the door for her and escorted her to the front porch.

On the drive home it might have nagged at another man that he should have tried for a good-night kiss, but I worried about whether my foster brother, Lee, would lend me his car again. I couldn't borrow Dad's. On weekends he was a part-time bartender at the Bachelor Officer's Quarters at the Naval Receiving Station, which was a bit like Willie Sutton serving as a bank teller, only with Dad dipping into the whiskey rather than the till. So I had to depend on the kindness of a sixteen-year-old boy, a rich kid who lived under the same roof as me but might as well have been a prince slumming it among peasants. When his brother, Wayne, had killed their adoptive parents, Lee had inherited the family's estate, a legacy of several hundred thousand dollars. He never lacked a car, clothing or pocket money, and fortunately for me, he had a sense of noblesse oblige. Without his generosity my courtship of Adrienne Daly would have foundered before it began.

The next night, returning to Bethesda, I took note of the neighborhood. The colonnade of trees along Adrienne's street. The Cadillacs, Lincolns and Chryslers gleaming in driveways. A lifelong resident of tract houses in the raw suburbs of Prince Georges County, I regarded this community as the epitome of luxury.

Still, I wasn't so dazzled that I didn't notice something odd about the Daly house. A white-stuccoed Spanish Provincial with a tile roof, it stood out amid the shingled Cape Cods and red-brick colonials like an illegal alien at a DAR convention. The front yard was ill tended, the vegetation overgrown, the lawn tufted with weeds in some spots and bald in others. And the family Cadillac, with its extravagant fins, needed a good polishing and some body work.

Adrienne let me in, then left me in the foyer while she bustled off to say good-bye to her parents. I heard their voices at the rear of the house. The Dalys didn't bother to come out, as most girls' folks would have done, if only to give the fellow a once-over. So I had a chance to look around the living room.

I had expected to be impressed, to think, Ah, so that's how the rich live. Adrienne's father was supposed to be a big shot in the government and her mother a Maryland politico. But their home had a decor indistinguishable in my eyes from the oriental bric-a-brac you saw in the house of every army vet who had served in the Far East. The oriental carpets, the Chinese screens inlaid with mother-of-pearl dragons, the wall hangings of geishas and willow trees may have been priceless originals, but they looked like cheap imitations to me.

Adrienne returned to the foyer, holding out a small overnight bag, not much bigger than a pocketbook. Was I supposed to admire it? No, she expected me to carry its featherweight to the car. I was glad to.

"Hope you don't mind," she said as we drove off. "We had Korean food for dinner, and I reek of garlic."

"I love garlic," I said, and ever since then I have. For Proust, the taste of a *petite madeleine* prompted remembrances of things past. For me, garlic does the trick.

"That's good," she said. "Not everybody does. When I was a little

girl, my family was driving in California and eating kimchi. A police-
man pulled us over for speeding, and when Daddy rolled down the
window, the smell of garlic rushed out, and the cop let us go with a
warning. He was that desperate to get away."

"I don't mind it," I swore.

"Still, don't count on any kissing," she said, her flirtatiousness too
theatrical to be taken seriously.

For the second night running, we wound up at an art-house film, a
black-and-white British import called *The L-Shaped Room*. Neither of us
knew a thing about it except that it starred Leslie Caron, the gamine
French actress who had won an Oscar for *Gigi*. I feel obliged to empha-
size the randomness of our movie choice. Otherwise its plot is bound to
seem like a calculated piece of foreshadowing that no self-respecting
writer would inflict on a reader.

Sad and forlorn, Leslie Caron leaves Paris for London and pitches up
in a seedy rooming house. Another lodger, a young novelist finishing his
first book, hears her retching with morning sickness. Leslie admits she's
pregnant and tells him the baby's father is a sailor. They took no precau-
tions, she says. That would have ruined the romance. Now she doesn't
want to marry the man and is unsure what to do.

The writer falls in love with her, as I knew I would have done—
lavishing affection on Leslie Caron in exchange for her tender encouragement with my work. Under normal circumstances, I'd have no chance
with a woman that beautiful, but if she were in trouble, she might turn
to me, and I'd give her all I had.

The novelist suggests they get married and raise the baby as their
own. This forces Leslie to reveal more than she'd like. The sailor was
black. She can't ask the novelist to pretend to be the father.

The writer pressures Leslie to have an abortion. Afterward they can start over; it'll be a new beginning. "Except," as Leslie points out, "it would be the end." Still, she pays a sleazy doctor sixty guineas for some pills that are supposed to cause a miscarriage. They make her sick, but she doesn't lose the baby. Relieved, she decides to carry it to term.

Much as he loves her, the novelist can't bear it. No matter that Leslie proclaims, "You're the first man I've ever loved. . . . Nothing matters except you and me." He hates it that she has a child growing inside her that's no part of him. The pain of this, piled atop mounting disappointment about his work, drives him away from Leslie.

The other lodgers look after her. Several matronly prostitutes and their kindly johns buck up her spirits as Christmas and her due date draw near. One sweet hooker says, "I hope you have a girl. They're less trouble than boys really."

Leslie does have a girl. The writer visits mother and child in the hospital, but regrets that he can't find it in him to stay with her. Leslie tells him, "You have nothing to be sorry about. Without you I might not have had the baby." In the end she returns to Paris to raise her daughter.

As the credits scrolled over the screen, Adrienne Daly did an extraordinary thing. She leaned her face into her hands and sobbed. I could not have been more deeply moved had she declared her love for me. Accustomed to women breaking down and crying, I was at home with sadness as I was with no other emotion. There's no telling how long it might have taken me to get around to touching Adrienne, but when she burst into tears, I instinctively reached over and rubbed her shoulders. I continued caressing her until she dried her eyes and I no longer had an excuse to have my hands on her.

As we walked to the car, she said, "I apologize for being so weepy. You're sweet to put up with me."

"Not at all. It was a sad movie."

"More sentimental than sad. Luckily, the ending saved it. Things worked out as they had to."

I disagreed. "He should have stayed with her. They could have married and moved to Paris together."

"Oh boy, what a romantic."

"No, I'm being realistic. She was the best thing in his sorry life. He was nuts to let her go. He'll never find anyone like her."

"They would have made each other miserable," she said.

"He's going to be miserable anyhow."

"He'll get over it. He got a novel out of the affair. He'll be fine."

"He'll need more than that to get over her."

"What did you want? A happy Hollywood ending?"

Insulted, I argued that it wasn't naive to believe they could have been happy together.

Adrienne shrugged. "I don't care whether I'm happy. I just don't want to live a boring, predictable life."

By the time I had unlocked the car door for her and come around to the other side, Adrienne was crying again. I slid in behind the wheel and stroked the nape of her neck, just below the soft coil of her chignon. "There, there, there," I crooned, as my grandmother used to when I cried as a kid.

"This is so embarrassing," she said. "I'm not like this."

I wanted to take her in my arms and kiss the tears from her cheeks. But I didn't push my luck.

"What about you?" she asked. "Would you rather have a boring, happy life? Or a sad, interesting one?"

I thought my life had already been interesting enough and that I might benefit from a bit of happiness. But because I sensed that that wasn't what Adrienne cared to hear, I claimed that I favored tragedy.

CHAPTER SEVEN

I
t would be a simplification to say that I fell in love with Adrienne Daly. What I felt seemed closer to sickness, and my desire was indistinguishable from despair. My chances of success with her, always a long shot, put me in a state of perpetual tension. Anxious about my clothing, my looks, my lack of a car, I decided that money was the answer. How to get it was the question.

For a while I worked on weekends, cleaning offices in downtown D.C. This was a source of shame to Tommy, whose mother had supported her family as a charwoman. My boss, Mr. Bradford, gave me a ride to and from the job, picking me up and dropping me off on Kenilworth Avenue so that I had to walk only a mile each way. He piled on the hours and led me to believe I was accumulating quite a bundle in overtime.

But on payday I waited two hours in the wind, and he never showed up. His office number rang and rang. At his home, his wife said she knew nothing about his business; she'd pass along a message. When he didn't call back, I kept dialing his house until I finally reached him. Mr. Bradford maintained that he was strapped for cash. When he had some money, I'd get mine. Like it or lump it.

I decided to lump it. Enraged, I drove Lee's car to Mr. Bradford's and stole the wrought-iron lawn furniture from his front yard. By phone, I told him I'd return it as soon as he paid me. Mr. Bradford bellowed about grand larceny, extortion, bribery. If he called the cops, as he threatened to, I'd be in jail next semester, not in college. But he capitulated.

"Now how am I going to feed my family?" he demanded as he handed me a brown envelope.

While he wrestled the lawn chairs out of Lee's car, I counted the money. By my reckoning, it was fifty bucks short. "Where's the overtime?" I asked.

"I promised you a dollar and a quarter an hour. Show me where it's written I'd pay time and a half."

What could I do? Swipe the furniture again? Belt him? I drove away feeling whipped, powerless and, as usual, poor.

Looking back, I realize I was reenacting the time-worn plot of many a film and a favorite theme of country music: boy from the wrong side of the tracks meets girl to the manor born, and their romance runs neither straight nor true. But I hadn't been down this road before and had no practice at bracing myself for the bumps and curves.

Since we were enrolled in the same Renaissance literature course, Adrienne and I saw each other several times a week. Beyond that, I could count on nothing. She had a full dance card. Some weekends, she flew off to Boston or New Haven. She once asked me to drive her to the airport so she could attend a cotillion at Columbia University. I told her to go to hell; I wasn't about to make it easy for her to date other guys.

She accused me of being childish. In that era of early marriages and earlier engagements, it was considered fair to play the field until you were formally spoken for. As a sophomore, Adrienne had been pinned— or engaged to be engaged—to an older fellow named Dave, an army vet who had now graduated. Although she had returned his pin, and they no longer had an exclusive relationship, she still went out with Dave and had to fit in our dates around ones with him.

Then Dave started to pop up everyplace Adrienne and I went. I took this as a personal affront, an attempt to intimidate me. He was a big guy, with short blond hair combed across a sunburned scalp. I sized him up, wondering whether things might take a rancorous turn, then speculated that his red-rimmed eyes might be grief-stricken rather than angry. He said nothing, just stared longingly at Adrienne.

Although I had never been down this particular road before, I had once taken a stroll on a similar path. The year before I had worked after school as a cashier at Safeway. The great thing about checking groceries, some people said, was that you didn't have to think. The worst thing, I found, was that you really couldn't think. My brain shorted out, and my feet fell asleep. To relieve the boredom, a fellow checker, a French major, practiced speaking *la belle langue* to me. But the manager warned him to knock it off. It upset the customers.

The doors closed at 9 P.M. Stragglers shopped until the lights dimmed at 10, and after we counted our tills and turned in the day's receipts, it was too late to go out with most girls. In my art history class, however, there was a night owl named Marisa who didn't mind a late date. Haughty and attractive in the enameled fashion of Jackie Kennedy, she suggested that I pose for her life drawing class. Though university regulations mandated that models wear swimming suits, she said students were free to sketch what they imagined lay beneath. I lied that I wouldn't do it unless I could be naked.

Marisa had a different guy for the early shift. She professed to be torn between us. Though jealous, I didn't care to lose her—even if it was unclear in what sense I had her. Whenever I tried to kiss her, she swiveled her head like Linda Blair in *The Exorcist,* leaving me to chew a mouthful of hair.

When the early-shift suitor started to stalk us, I thought it added spice to our dates. "How can you take him seriously?" I chortled. "He's a clown."

But one evening while I was punching cash-register keys at Safeway, the fellow punched Marisa. He beat her up so badly she had to be hospitalized. I assumed this ended the competition, and I had won.

I was dead wrong. Being coldcocked brought clarity to Marisa's life. She realized how deeply she loved the lout. They married almost immediately and six months later had a baby. Afterward I brooded that I had been a catalyst—worse, an irrelevance—in their romance.

So when Dave began to lurk in the background, I kept my eyes open and my guard up. On February 25, 1964, Adrienne invited me to a play, a student production of *Beaux Stratagem.* I recall the date because it was the night of the first Cassius Clay–Sonny Liston fight. During the play I kept a transistor radio in my pocket and an earphone plugged into my ear. It appalled Adrienne that I liked boxing and would prefer a fight to a Restoration comedy. After the curtain call, she left the theater while I sat listening to the eighth and climactic round.

When Liston slumped on his stool and refused to answer the bell, it was for me as though the accepted order of the universe had flipped upside down. If a young loudmouth upstart not much older than I could whip the invincible Big Bear . . . why, anything was possible. Drunk with astonishment and fizzing with adrenaline, I hurried to catch up with Adrienne.

She was in the lobby, huddled in conversation with Dave, my personal Big Bear. For a moment, I hung back. Then in shame I thought of Cassius Clay, the new heavyweight champ, who by morning would become Muhammad Ali, thumbing his nose at the white world. Would he hesitate? Not on your life!

I sailed across the lobby, not truculent or itching for trouble, just sure of myself. I told Dave that when he had a date with Adrienne, I'd stay out of his way. When I had a date with her, I expected him to do the same.

He didn't answer, didn't look at me. He gazed at Adrienne, waiting, I guessed, for her to make up her mind. Or did he intend to sucker punch me? When I took her elbow, there was tension in her arm. For an instant, it seemed possible that she might stay with him. But then she walked away with me, and once we were outside the building, she slipped her hand into my coat pocket and intertwined her fingers with mine.

"Who won?" she asked.

"Clay," I said. "I can't wait for the rematch."

Would that our other differences were as easy to deal with as Dave. I was a Catholic, and that seemed a bad idea to her. I wanted to be a novelist, and while she admired writing, she believed it was something best done after a successful career in a different field. She cited the example of statesmen, generals and actors who publish memoirs late in life.

To be fair, much of the friction might have been chalked up to cultural misunderstandings. Prickly about my shortcomings and eager to impress her, I invited Adrienne to one of my intramural basketball games. Here was something I thought I did as well as anybody except the fellows on the varsity. But she said I acted like a hoodlum on court. She hated my scowling mug, my nonstop hustle, which she regarded as hostility, and my legs, which were more muscular and hairier than she liked. "You want to win so badly," she summed it up, "and you're so obvious about it."

The first time Adrienne and I ate dinner together in a restaurant, as opposed to a coffee shop or hamburger joint, I watched and tried to follow her example in the perilous challenge of knife, fork and napkin usage. But, rushing ahead of myself, I rashly dug into the butter dish, slathered a slab of bread and plunked the knife down on the tablecloth.

With the forbearance of a mother instructing an obstinate child, Adrienne demonstrated what I should have done. Speared a single pat of butter. Placed it on the bread plate. Broken off a bite-sized morsel of bread. Spread the butter on the bread. Then laid the knife, just so, on the edge of the plate.

Face burning with trailer-park pride, I picked up my knife and plunked it down on the tablecloth again.

"Don't do that," she said patiently. "You'll stain the tablecloth."

"Adrienne," I said and paused until I had her full attention, "fuck the tablecloth."

"Oh, I see," she said, "you're rehearsing for *Streetcar Named Desire*. You're playing Stanley Kowalski."

It embarrasses me that I couldn't bring myself to laugh. A failed sense of humor is unforgivable. But Adrienne didn't appear to mind, at least not enough to give up on me. She persisted in her role as educator and social arbiter, and I flattered myself that we must be linked by some powerful sexual chemistry, like Lady Chatterley and Mellors the gamekeeper. So what if as yet we had done no more than hold hands?

At that point, the most intimate connection between us was words, language, our mutual love of talking. I wrote her letters. I passed her notes in class. We spent hours on the phone. After twenty-one years of *omertà* during which I had never felt free to discuss my parents' divorce, my stepfather's disastrous drinking or my mother's depression, much less my own emotions, I now hemorrhaged a stream of secrets. And to my shock, Adrienne didn't just listen. She encouraged me. She empathized. In a sense, she was my first literary acceptance.

To my far greater surprise, she responded in kind. She described her troubled family. A father whose career was in decline. A mother whose expectations kept rising. A black-sheep brother. A childhood of feast or famine in foreign countries. "I remember times," Adrienne told me, "when we lived in a mansion with seven servants. Then we had nothing, and the next thing I knew we were on a steamer in the South China Sea being shot at by pirates."

She explained that she had entered the Miss Maryland contest because it offered college scholarships and financial opportunities. Sometimes when she couldn't see me, she was speaking to groups that paid to have Miss Prince Georges County grace their gatherings. This was better, she said, than doing what she had done before—selling encyclopedias door to door and peddling memberships to Vic Tanny's gym.

The more I heard, the more I felt sorry for her and the closer I believed we were becoming. If I had a lot to learn, and a lot of rough edges to round off, Adrienne wasn't without her neediness too. But it didn't occur to me that she might crave something more than care and attention and talk. It didn't occur to me that she might find me physically attractive—and very slow to read the signals.

The night before the midterm exam in Renaissance literature, Adrienne and I had a study date. Behind in my reading, I needed to catch up. Since I had a key to the *Calvert Review* office, empty at night, we went there for privacy and quiet. At least we would have had quiet if Adrienne hadn't been in a quirky, agitated mood. Complaining that I was ignoring her, she started declaiming aloud from *Utopia*. Then, in a switch to poetry, she quoted one of Wyatt's sonnets: "They flee from me that sometime did me seek / with naked foot stalking in my chamber." She added as if it were a rhyming couplet, "I bet if I wanted to leave this room, you couldn't stop me."

"Nobody's forcing you to stay."

"What I mean is, you couldn't hold me here against my will. You're not strong enough."

"Don't bet on it."

"You're all talk." She set down her notebook.

"I'm afraid I'll hurt you."

"I think you're afraid, period."

Seeing her poised to run, I put my notebook aside. As she broke for the door, I pounced, grabbing her before she had gone two steps. The firmness of her body, its wriggling solidity, her ferocious determination to wrench free astounded me. Though she laughed, she was dead set on escaping. If I didn't get a better grip, she would leave me holding air.

I locked my arms around her waist, lifted her off her feet and turned her upside down. Her head hung close to the floor. Her chignon uncoiled in a shower of bobby pins, and as she thrashed back and forth, her long hair swept the tiles. I was terrified of dropping her.

Still she struggled, unafraid of falling. She fought as if her life, her love, something essential depended upon it. In slacks and a pullover, she didn't care about ripping her clothes. Scissoring her legs around my neck, she yanked at my knees. I staggered and had trouble knowing where I dared touch her. Finally my hands went everywhere, but unable to control her, I tripped, and the two of us toppled over in a tangle of limbs.

That should have jolted us to our senses, but Adrienne wouldn't quit. She squirmed beneath me, and as we grappled and heaved like a couple of Greco-Roman wrestlers, I wondered whether she was crazy. Or was I? I knew it didn't matter who won. Still, I wouldn't give up. I flipped her onto her back and pinned her shoulders with my knees. Adrienne arched her spine, trying to throw me off. When she couldn't do it, she smiled as though she, not I, were on top. "You're not so big and tough as you think you are," she taunted me.

"Tough enough to take you."

"Yeah, but I'm just a girl," she simpered.

"That's right. Don't forget it."

I let her up, and we stood facing each other, breathing hard as we straightened our clothes. When she crouched to pick up her hairpins, I knelt beside her and helped. To my shame, my hands were shaking. Not wanting her to notice, I told her I was going to the men's room to towel off and have a drink of water.

The fluorescent-lit mirror above the sink highlighted the red streaks on my neck where Adrienne's slacks had roughed up the skin. I looked like somebody who had been cut down from a noose. But I felt suffused with the dreamy tenderness of sexual arousal or its aftermath.

Back in the *Calvert Review* office, Adrienne was replaiting her hair, winding it into a chignon. She kept her eyes averted, and in a distracted voice she told me that she had signed out of the sorority house overnight. I could take her home, she said, or . . . or someplace else.

U.S. Highway 1 cut through the University of Maryland, and for miles in either direction it was lined with motels. Even if I had had the money—which I didn't—it wouldn't have dawned on me to suggest checking into one, nor did I believe there was any chance that Adrienne would agree. That's how green I was.

I told her I had a friend with an off-campus apartment. She grimaced. She preferred privacy. But since there was no choice, she didn't argue. My friend supplied pillows and sheets, then disappeared into his bedroom while Adrienne and I arranged a bed of cushions on the living room floor. The apartment had one saving grace—a fireplace where I built a small blaze of sticks and rolled newspapers.

Adrienne pulled out her bobby pins and placed them on an end table so she could find them in the morning. Her hair, when she shook it loose, hung to her waist. Without undressing, she lay down on the sheet, and her hair fanned out against the pillow.

I stretched out beside her and combed my fingers through her hair. Then I kissed her ear. I might have stopped there if she hadn't pressed her mouth to mine. In those days, sexual terrain was explored in slow, minute increments. At least it was by me. She kissed me, and I kissed her back, and for the rest of the night that was pretty much all we did. Her hands remained on my shoulders, mine on the small of her back. We touched no place else except our lips and tongues, suspended for hours in a sort of Tantric out-of-body state that constituted the best sex I'd never had.

In the morning, over breakfast at a waffle shop, Adrienne's mouth and chin were chapped from kissing. Since I still had red marks on my neck, the waitress might have imagined that we had been through a bout of rough sex. Adrienne thanked me for not pushing her too far, too fast. That, she said, would have ruined everything. She swore she had never felt closer to anybody than she had last night. Then she told me she loved me.

That was that, I assumed. We were a couple. But the following weekend, she flew to New York again. She claimed that she couldn't get out of an invitation from old friends, a married couple who lived in suburban Mamaroneck and had recently had a baby. Though she made it sound like a dreary domestic obligation, I didn't show much graciousness about her going away, nor did I volunteer to drive her to the airport.

When I saw her on Monday, she said that her hosts had treated her to dinner at a famous Manhattan restaurant. She mentioned its name as if I should recognize it. She wondered whether we would ever spend a romantic weekend in New York, and if we did, would I know how to order wine?

Then she suggested that we spend the day on her grandmother's farm, out in the Maryland countryside. Like her parents' house, the place surprised me, both because of its disrepair and its setting. A large white antebellum home located on acres of open meadow, it had a pond and a hardwood forest at its fringes. But any impression of baronial splendor, past or present, was undermined by the shrill harmonics of a nearby highway and the tracks of the B&O railroad, which ran within earshot of the front door. Adding visual insult to acoustic injury, a junkyard sprawled along one boundary of the property.

Adrienne's grandmother was as baffling as her farm. Though the matriarch of a family of wealth and prominence—one of her close relatives was a senior senator in Washington—she dressed in drab, patchwork clothes. She had recently been kicked by a horse and was in excruciating pain from a broken shoulder, but she refused to see a doctor. She was a Christian Scientist and believed in mending the bone through prayer and meditation.

After commiserating with her, Adrienne told her grandmother that we were here to study, and she led me upstairs to a sewing room that had a foldout bed. She removed her blouse and bra and showed me a thread-thin scar on her breast. As I traced it with my fingertip, she said she had gotten it as a little girl falling out of an apple tree. As she grew, the scar had grown, curving into a lazy question mark. For me the story had the plangency of a ballad, the allusiveness of biblical allegory.

I kissed the scar. I kissed that breast, then the other. When I started to unzip her slacks, she said, "No. Not yet." I stopped, satisfied that we had all the time in the world.

. . .

On the trip back to the campus, she talked about her sorority's annual spring dance. This year's theme, the country club locale, the decorating committee, the cost per couple. Just as I expected her to produce an engraved invitation, Adrienne said that she had asked Dave to take her. She claimed to be doing me a favor, saving me the expense of tickets, a corsage and tux rental.

Too furious to drive, I skidded off the road and into an abandoned Amoco station that had yellow crime-scene tape garlanding the gas pumps. Too furious to speak, I sat there buffeted by the backwash of trucks hurtling toward Washington and Baltimore.

"What's wrong?" she asked in a voice of meek amazement. "It's just a prom. I mean, I don't even know whether you like to dance."

"I don't," I said flatly. "I don't dance. I don't know a damn thing about wine. And I don't want to see you again."

"Why?" she wailed.

"I'm fed up. You say you love me. You tell me you've never felt closer to anybody. You must think I'm a fool, someone you can string along until you get a better offer."

Adrienne slid across the front seat and took my face between her cool palms. "I do love you. I thought you loved me and understood that I'm just marking time, waiting for you to graduate."

"What are you talking about?"

"I thought—excuse the presumption—I thought . . ." She shook her head, and tears swam in her eyes. "I thought I'd get a job this June after I graduate, and then by the time you finish next spring, I'll have enough saved for us to get married. The rest of this, the dances and so forth, are just time filler."

Delighted, I did an abrupt 180-degree turn. This was how things often happened in our day. People married right out of college, and the wife worked while hubby was in the army or grad school. Although I didn't picture myself becoming a happy home owner in the suburbs, I welcomed the thought of a wife's company and support as I established myself as a novelist.

Adrienne was on my lap now, in my arms, her hands still clasping my face. "Promise me one thing," she said. "Promise me you won't get disgusted and leave me."

"Why would I do that?"

"I just need to know you won't."

"I promise."

CHAPTER EIGHT

A few weeks later, when Adrienne confessed that she was pregnant, alternating currents of pain and panic surged through me. Against all reason—we still hadn't gotten beyond the petting stage—I felt it was my fault. If not for something I had done, then for something I had failed to do. But what?

Where I was raised, the way I was raised, the protocol in such cases was strict. If a woman cheated, a man dumped her, but not before doling out a wicked tongue-lashing or worse. Yet I stayed on, overpowered by contradictory impulses. Along with anger and disbelief, I felt something akin to resignation that gradually shaded into relief.

Of course she's pregnant, I thought. As I had intuited when watching *The L-Shaped Room,* something would have to be wrong before I had a chance with a woman like Leslie Caron—or Adrienne Daly. But rather than self-pity, this recognition brought on a strange elation. My life was opening up, not narrowing, and among the new possibilities for a boy of my bookish nature was the thrill of being swept up into an absorbing narrative.

Two of my novels, *Waking Slow* and *True Crime,* published twenty years apart, contain scenes based on Adrienne's announcement of her pregnancy. In neither, however, did I manage to capture the absurd comedy that ran at cross-purposes with the melodrama. Only a twenty-one-year-old as earnest as I was then would fail to appreciate the inherent humor of the situation.

It was a warm April afternoon, and we were sitting in front of Adrienne's sorority house in a Fiat Bianchina, the smallest automobile manufactured in Italy. As usual, I had borrowed a car, and for this occasion I had come up with a court jester's jitney, the sort of vehicle a dozen clowns might tumble out of at a circus. Three short months before, having seen *The L-Shaped Room,* I had sworn to Adrienne that I preferred tragedy. Yet here I was, in a parody of that film, playing a straight man, the butt of the joke.

Many years later I experienced a jolt of recognition and roared with laughter when I read in Philip Roth's *American Pastoral:* "You wanted Miss America? Well, you've got her now, with a vengeance. You longed to belong like everybody else in the USA. Well now you do." Having laid siege to the lady, fearing the whole time that I was soiling her with my filthy paws, I found myself saddled with the gypsy's curse—careful what you pray for.

When I asked who the lucky guy was, Adrienne admitted it was Dave. When I demanded, How? When? Where? Why? she decried my mania for pinning her down. Citing as she often did her favorite film, *Rashomon,* she reminded me of the relativity of truth. In the movie four characters witness a rape—was she implying that Dave had taken her against her will?—and draw four different conclusions. Since the damage was done, what did the rest of it matter? she asked.

It mattered to me. The devil was in the details. On them depended my capacity to understand and my willingness to forgive.

She started off leading me to believe that she had been pregnant when we met. But it soon became apparent that this couldn't be true. She had missed just one period. It had happened little more than a month ago in New York. Dave had driven her to the airport, bought a ticket and barged onto the shuttle. Though she acknowledged that they had occasionally been intimate in the past, she swore they had stopped having sex before she and I started dating. But over that weekend, he kept pressuring her.

"I thought you were staying with friends in Mamaroneck," I said. "Was Dave there?"

"Yes, they were his friends too. He wouldn't leave me alone. He told me he was taking an experimental contraceptive for men. It was supposed to raise his body temperature and kill sperm. He said I couldn't possibly get pregnant. In the end, he wore me down."

She recounted all this without a flicker of irony, and I accepted it without a snicker of sarcasm. I did give vent to my anger, but it was aimed at Dave for badgering Adrienne, tricking her. What a bastard he had been!

"What are you going to do?" I asked.

"I'm not sure."

"Have you told Dave?"

"Yes."

"What's he say?"

"He wants to marry me." This was what couples in trouble did in 1964—a hurried shotgun wedding. But Adrienne said, "I don't want to marry him. I don't love Dave. I love you."

I remember glancing into the Fiat's rearview mirror, as if a solution lay somewhere behind us. "If you love me . . ."

"Why did I do it?" she broke in with a question I might well have asked. "How could I possibly get pregnant when I love you? I can't explain, Mike. I don't understand it myself."

"If you love me," I repeated, "we could get married and raise the baby as ours."

"It wouldn't work. I can't ask that of you, Mike. It wouldn't be fair."

To this day I wonder what I would have done if she had agreed. I think I would have married her. It seemed to me that she wouldn't have confided that she was pregnant if she didn't expect something from me. So I said I'd help.

"I'm considering an abortion," she said. "Do you know how to get one?"

I didn't. Maybe she believed that with my low-rent roots, I had access to anything illegal. Plenty of girls in my neighborhood got pregnant, but I knew of no one who had had an abortion. And although Adrienne thought otherwise, it wasn't simply because I was Catholic that I told her I wouldn't ask around. I'd have had no idea where to start.

She changed directions so quickly that I question whether she had been serious about an abortion. Our discussion turned to the alternative—putting the baby up for adoption. In that day, usually because men refused to do the right thing, women withdrew to homes or convents for unwed mothers. Girls of my acquaintance who had gone through this described a Dickensian world of harsh discipline and isolation. These institutions seemed to view it as their mission to exact as much shame as possible.

Adrienne wanted no part of such a place. Neither did I. She emphasized that after graduation, she needed to disappear before she started to show. Her family and friends must never know she was pregnant. Since she and a sorority sister intended to travel to San Francisco this summer to volunteer at the Republican Party convention, she mused that at four months she might be slender enough to escape unnoticed. Afterward she could stay in California without causing suspicion. She would tell her parents that she was going to give the West Coast a try. Once the baby was born in late December, she would move back East.

I pictured her living in a dingy bedsitter like the one in *The L-Shaped Room*. How she would work, how she'd support herself, I couldn't envision. As distraught as she was now, I hated to think of what she would face in the coming months alone. I also hated to think how I would deal day to day with her absence, three thousand miles away, needing medical attention, needing money, needing love.

A cynic might accuse me of latching onto any excuse to stay with her, any reason to believe that she had made an uncharacteristic error and that Dave had taken advantage of her. But at a deeper level, I sensed that this setback might represent an opportunity. Having inherited my mother's bipolar tendencies, I tried to regard every trauma as a trampoline that would turn my luck around.

When I offered to join her in San Francisco as soon as the convention ended and her girlfriend left, Adrienne accepted the suggestion as if everything had been preordained and we had planned this just as many of her sorority sisters were planning their June weddings.

For the rest of that semester, I proceeded as if nothing had changed. I submitted a novella for the campus literary prize and lost out to my friend Tom. With the encouragement of the current editor and faculty adviser, I applied for the editorship of the *Calvert Review* and won the appointment. I notified the Selective Service Board that I needed an extension of my student military deferment for my senior year. To ensure that I could drop out during the fall semester and still graduate on time, I registered for two summer courses—colonial American literature and introduction to philosophy. Then, to pay for the move west and an apartment and medical care for Adrienne, I looked for a job.

I landed one at Pepsi-Cola, driving a truck and delivering cases of soda. It was backbreaking labor, and as Adrienne advised me, although it might beef up my biceps, it wouldn't add muscle to my résumé. After two weeks, I quit and signed on at the Marriott Corporation as a "food service management trainee." To get the job, I lied just as I had with Pepsi, claiming that I was married and that my wife was about to have a baby.

After an orientation period at Marriott's headquarters, where the top corporate people hailed from Utah and most of the new hires came out of Cornell University's hotel and restaurant school, I was assigned to a Hot Shoppe in Anacostia, not far from the Naval Receiving Station. For long hours, I practiced breading onion rings, frying cheeseburgers and whipping up desserts whose toppings were sprayed from a container labeled "Industrial Dairy By-Product." Waiters had to serve these desserts promptly, before the ersatz whipped cream dissolved into its chemical constituents. In the afternoon, the Hot Shoppe manager and I huddled in his office to review recipes and discuss company philosophy. Then I dashed off to the university to lectures on Cotton Mather and Descartes.

For graduation, Adrienne's parents bought her a Ford Thunderbird, and whenever I didn't have night classes, we'd tool around Washington in this sleek metallic-gray roadster. For somebody who had recently been at the wheel of a lumbering Pepsi truck, it was a heady experience driving a T-bird—even if I did sometimes have to pull over to the curb and let Adrienne toss her cookies in the gutter. She suffered awful morning sickness and was exhausted from packing for her trip. She complained that I didn't give her room to breathe. But in the next instant she'd break into tears and beg me to hold her tight.

The day Adrienne set off for San Francisco, I stood at the steam table at the Hot Shoppe, and while ladling up meat in an iridescent sauce, I noticed a roach tightrope up an electrical cord and squeeze into a wall clock through its winding stem. Far from a refuge, the clock face was a dangerous spot. As a blood-red second hand swept down on it like a scimitar, the insect scuttled in a circle, frantic to escape. I identified with the roach and felt I was running helter-skelter with a blade at my neck. I didn't dare slow down and look back.

Toward the end of the Republican convention, before Barry Goldwater delivered his acceptance speech as the party's presidential candidate, Adrienne called to say that San Francisco was a mistake. For a second, I thought she meant to have the baby on her own. But she said she had seen old friends there and had made a few new ones, and was afraid she'd bump into them again when she was big as a blimp. Would I mind meeting her in Los Angeles? She knew nobody there and thought the city's anonymous sprawl would serve our purposes better. That was fine by me.

By mid-August, as I rolled up one life and readied myself for another, I felt like a prisoner who carves a wax replica to leave on his bunk while he burrows through the wall with a sharpened spoon. Telling lie after lie, I shucked off my old identity and cloaked myself in a new one. Creating a fictional life gave me giddy insight into how that Student Union imposter, the one who had pretended to be progressing toward a degree right up until he stuck a pistol into his mouth, must have felt. This was fun, exhilarating, slightly scary, but not bad as long as you didn't look down.

I told school friends I was moving to California for literary motives; to become a writer I needed to experiment. Resigning from the *Calvert Review* editorship, I claimed that an aging uncle in LA had fallen ill and I had to care for him. I used the same excuse with the Selective Service Board, which guaranteed that I wouldn't be drafted as long as I graduated next spring. To quit the Marriott Corporation, however, required a more convincing story. I called my boss late at night and said my wife, now almost five months pregnant, had had an accident in California. She and the baby would survive, but since she needed rehabilitative surgery and couldn't be moved for the foreseeable future, I had to relocate to be with her during the long convalescence.

At home, Mom was in one of her periodic up cycles. For days she didn't sleep, seldom stopped talking, rarely quit cleaning the house, tending her rosebushes and planning projects that she would abandon during the next depression. In manic phases, she was hyperalert and missed little that happened in the house. Immediately sensing something askew about my mood, she dogged me with questions. "I know something's wrong," she said. "Tell me what it is." Then she leaped to her own conclusion. "Your girlfriend's pregnant."

I didn't deny it. There was no point in lying. I was too upset to maintain the deception, and she was too relentless in pursuit of the truth. When I told her that I wasn't the father, she seemed neither surprised nor dubious. Her instant response was, "You have to help her." From this it was a short step to her saying, "Maybe I should adopt the baby." I cut that off, telling her we were going west to give the baby up for adoption. "Yes, that's best," she agreed. "You've got to show her lots of love."

As for Dad, I'm tempted to say he was drinking more than ever. But who could keep count? The night before I left for California, he staggered to my room—to say good-bye, I guessed. It was hard to tell. He was almost incoherent. He tried to hug me, as he had when I was a little boy, but I was now six inches taller than he. Leaning his head against my chest, he babbled that he hurt, he hurt all over. He saw bugs on his arms and legs, on the walls and ceiling, in his hair. He knew they weren't real. He hadn't gone nuts. But he felt them crawling on his skin, under his skin, inside him.

Rocking him in my arms, I whispered for him to get a grip on himself and prayed that I wouldn't lose mine. His sweat smelled like scotch whiskey, his hair like cigarette smoke. I walked him to the family room and seated him in front of the TV, where a preseason NFL game was in progress. Years later, as he lay dying in a hospital bed hooked up to tubes and wires, incoherent from cancer, I did the same thing. I tuned in a football game for him, then tiptoed out of his life, half-sick with hopeless love for him, half-sick and ashamed of my hatred.

CHAPTER NINE

Eager to economize, I didn't consider catching a train or plane to the West Coast. Since it cost over $100, even a Greyhound bus was out of the question. Adrienne and I were going to need the money.

I would rather have hitchhiked. This was a trip I had made half a dozen times, thumbing across the United States. Back before interstates and national franchises flattened the experience, I loved traveling that way, surrendering to the narcotic of the open road, reveling in a sensation of absolute freedom. I remember hitchhiking to the Seattle World's Fair in 1961 and bedding down one night in the Horse Heaven Hills, whose deliciously alliterative name evokes the sweet essence of that summer, the immensity of the landscape with me pleasurably lost in it.

But now, short on time as well as money, I spotted an ad on the university bulletin board. A grad student heading west was looking for riders to share the driving and expenses. Luckily, I was his sole passenger.

Unluckily, he was in the history department and had the annoying habit of stopping at historical markers along the road. He insisted on reading them aloud and correcting errors of fact and interpretation.

Then, as we cruised through the heat warp of Oklahoma, he asked if I'd like to get laid. Here it goes, I thought. His hairy hand on my knee. A smarmy, throbbing proposition. But he was straight and said that at truck stops across the country, whores hung around tricking for johns. In midweek, in the middle of the day, he estimated that sex wouldn't cost more than $20.

When I told him I'd pass, he asked, Why? Was I queer or chicken?

I icily explained that pausing in the petroleum stink of a truck stop and screwing a twenty-dollar slag wasn't my idea of a Dionysian experience.

He guffawed. "I guess you'd prefer an Apollonian experience with some goody-two-shoes coed."

"I'd prefer to drop the subject."

He laughed louder. "I get it. You're a virgin."

"What if I am?" I snarled.

"Then there's something wrong with you."

"There's nothing wrong with me."

"Okay, you're just a case of arrested development. Let me treat you to a piece of ass. We'll pull over at the next place and be back on the road in no time."

Among my sexual fantasies, truck stops and prostitutes played no part. In this arena, as in many others, my inclinations were romantic, my appetites poetically pornographic. Paraphrasing Norman Mailer, I maintained that sex was an existential act and that any man who failed to infuse it with meaning could never make sense of life.

"Jesus, you really are fucked up," the grad student said. "You need a shrink, not a whore."

. . .

For the rest of the day, we drove in stony silence. On the outskirts of Albuquerque, I told him I'd travel the rest of the way to LA on my own. After he sped off, I phoned my father, and although he was surprised that I was in town, he sounded neither happy nor unhappy to hear from me. He said he'd pick me up in twenty minutes. That was plenty of time for me to practice referring to him as Dad, not Jack, and to remember that the man I usually called Dad had to be called Tommy.

My father's buzz-cut hair had gone solid white, and the high desert sun had pinkened his complexion. Otherwise, he was the same man I had never known. When he learned that I planned to skip the fall semester to live in Los Angeles, his reaction was that I was a fool. He said I couldn't expect him to continue paying child support while I larked around California.

I hadn't anticipated this. I doubted Mom had either. She was the one who cashed the check—$40 a month—and spent it as needed. I hated to think of her getting caught short, and I tried to persuade Jack—no, Dad!—that I'd be back in school for the second semester. As a matter of fact, if I maintained my current grade-point average, I would graduate Phi Beta Kappa.

"That and a dime will buy you a cup of coffee," he said. When was I going to get a brain in my head? He couldn't understand why I had quit the job as a Safeway cashier. If I had stayed on and kept paying union dues, I'd have been unfireable by now. I had to start living in the real world. I was twenty-one, too old for child support. That the money went to Mom, not me, made him more adamant about cutting off the payments.

In my father's defense, this was decades before children routinely heard the dulcet reassurance, "As long as you're happy, dear." "Happy" didn't count for much in that era, and from the perspective of many parents, my stated goal—to become a college professor—sounded like pie-in-the-sky nonsense. My secret goal—to become a novelist—would have prompted them to call in the men with nets and tranquilizers.

I left the next morning to hitchhike to LA. My father attempted to talk me out of it, but I wouldn't listen. Dug into my position—dug into my grave, he probably thought—I refused to accept advice, even sensible advice, from somebody who opposed every single thing that mattered to me. I did, however, let him drive me as far west as Gallup, where Indians from all over New Mexico had gathered for a tribal festival. He warned me not to ride with a drunk driver and offered to park nearby and keep an eye on me until I got a lift. I told him not to bother. That he might have wanted to spend a few last minutes watching his second-born son never crossed my mind.

Thirty hours later, sunburned and dust-spattered, I stood at the corner of La Cienega and Beverly Boulevards beside a sea bag stuffed with clothes and books. When Adrienne picked me up, she had a rich brown tan and had put on a few extra pounds. As she leaned forward to kiss me across the console between the T-bird's bucket seats, she joked that for the first time in her life, she had cleavage. Behind us, an impatient driver honked his horn, and Adrienne sped off, speaking in a rush, filling me in on her news.

Because she had been unsure about my arrival date—did this mean she had feared I wouldn't show up?—and because it was cheaper than a hotel, she was sharing an apartment with an older woman. "It's just till the end of the month. Just till we find a place."

"Does she know about me?"

"I told her my husband and I had separated and were reconciling."

I didn't get this, but before I could ask, she sprang a second surprise.

She had a job in the front office of a high-performance automobile company owned by the famous Formula One driver Carroll Shelby.

Our plan, I thought, had been to live together incognito, with me working and Adrienne arranging the adoption. Instead, to my bewilderment, she had a roommate and a celebrity boss but hadn't contacted a doctor or an adoption agency.

When I met the roommate—a loudmouthed, middle-aged alcoholic—and visited the apartment in a boisterous singles enclave that encircled a communal swimming pool, my confusion deepened. Had Adrienne changed her mind and decided not to bother hiding? Or was she in a clinical state of denial?

Because there was no space for me in the apartment, I spent the next week on Melrose Avenue, now an Eden of upscale boutiques and bistros, then a purgatory of shabby rooming houses. Mine was managed by an immensely fat woman with vaccination marks, like rivets, embedded in both shoulders. A prim landlady, she laid down the law—no alcohol, no smoking, no firearms and no sex on her premises. She demanded daily payment, and if I forgot to fork it over, she padlocked my room until I squared my account.

Each morning, Adrienne pulled up out front, an improbable flash of class in a luxury car that the landlady squinted at in befuddlement. After driving her to her job, I set off in the T-bird to find one of my own. Because I was unfamiliar with the city and feared that the convoluted intestinal tract of freeways would excrete me at a dead end in the desert, I stuck to secondary roads, those storied LA arteries clogged with hot-dog stands shaped like sausages and motels that resembled tepees, Kon-tiki huts, oriental pagodas, Swiss chalets and turreted castles.

My intention had been to plug in to some menial, low-stress position that would leave time for me to write and to sign up for a night course at UCLA. But Adrienne encouraged me to think about a good future reference. I didn't argue that novelists don't need references. In her hormonal state, we had enough disagreements. Increasingly, she didn't appear to be herself. Maybe it was just that her body belonged to the tiny creature that kicked and punched when I pressed my hand to Adrienne's belly.

Anyway, it wasn't difficult to find the sort of employment she recommended. Because so many young men were being inducted during the buildup in Vietnam, a twenty-one-year-old with no degree and a skimpy résumé, but with a wife and a baby on the way, and thus armor-plated against the draft, was regarded as a prime job candidate. Today, kids marrying early and having kids might sound idiotic, but back then they were considered to be demonstrating admirable maturity.

There was, however, one peculiar ritual that could undo an otherwise attractive applicant. Along with interviews and examinations—the Wunderlich to measure intelligence, the Minnesota Multiphasic Index to gauge emotional stability—I had to submit to a lie-detector test. Perhaps this was specific to LA in that paranoid epoch. I can't believe it's part of the current employment drill. I had wires attached to various parts of my body as I answered questions from a technician who monitored the polygraph. "Do you have a criminal record?" he asked. "A history of mental disease? Are you or have you ever been a member of the Communist Party or any organization that advocates the violent overthrow of the U.S. government?"

On important global issues, I passed with flying colors But the machine caught a pattern of deception about my married life. Was I running around on my wife? the technician asked with a leer and a laugh. I swore I wasn't. A bad case of nerves, I told him. Anxious to get the job, I was as tense as I had been on my wedding night, I said, as tense as I expected to be when the baby was born. This satisfied him.

Hired by Friden Inc., a subsidiary of the Singer Corporation, I sold business equipment, adding machines and calculators. Friden's most sophisticated product, an early-generation desktop computer, resembled a console TV, with a cathode-ray tube the size of a postcard. Primitive and slow as it was, I never mastered any of its functions. I was barely competent to switch it on and off. Nonetheless, I managed to persuade the Los Angeles County Road Department to invest in a top-of-the-line model, and for that I was named salesman of the month and awarded a Friden Inc. tie clasp.

Adrienne wasn't so fortunate. Like most women of that era, she was expendable in the marketplace, just attractive fluff. As soon as she started to show, she was fired. An expectant mother wasn't the image favored by a high-performance car company. The idea of equal rights and equal pay for women hadn't entered the national vocabulary.

Not accustomed to rejection and to having her talents go unrecognized, Adrienne was miffed. For a while, she accepted temporary secretarial work as a Kelly Girl. But that galled her too, and finally she stayed at home.

"Home" was a $125-a-month one-bedroom apartment on North Harper Street, a block south of Sunset Boulevard. It had no pool, no patio, no sundeck, no grace notes at all. We had budgeted for something better, but most rentals required a year's lease and local references. And in that day, when it wasn't so common for unmarried couples to live together, some landlords demanded documentary proof that tenants didn't violate California's statute forbidding "lewd cohabitation." In our cheap digs, we believed we were flying safely under the radar.

Once we had moved in, Adrienne lay in bed, resting, reading and smoking. Through the open windows filtered warm air, the scent of jasmine and the bump-and-grind beat of the Body Shop, a strip joint up on Sunset. It advertised an amateur contest every Tuesday night— C cups or better to qualify.

Stretched out beside Adrienne, I stared at the ashtray that she balanced on her belly. Every minute or so, the ashtray jiggled as the baby kicked. Then somebody knocked at the door, and the ashtray jumped.

"You get it," Adrienne whispered. There was worry on her face. We knew no one and couldn't guess who this might be.

I opened the door to a man who identified himself as the resident manager. "I got a bone to pick with you. We don't allow kids."

"We don't have kids," I said.

"Not now you don't. But I got eyes. The lady's five months along if she's a day. You didn't mention that."

"We didn't know about the rule."

"Read the lease. It's right in there."

I pleaded with him to let us stay until the baby's birth. After that, we'd find a new place. I couldn't bear to move now that we had settled.

"Okay," he said. "But meantime, anybody in the building asks, you tell them you're out of here the day she goes into labor."

After this early alarm, our improvised life subsided into a rhythm as regular as paydays and the rent. Every morning we woke to the singsong of Japanese gardeners who roved the neighborhood mowing lawns, pruning shrubbery and sweeping fragrant blossoms into wicker baskets. Like an extension of an East Coast summer, autumn in California was hot. Seasonal changes seemed suspended, and time didn't so much stop as elastically expand. We were waiting, and the weather waited with us. We were waiting not just for the baby but to see how things worked out between us. Adrienne, with her theatrical background, said we were waiting for Godot. We both began referring to the baby as Godot, although I don't believe either of us had in mind the bleakness of Beckett's play.

No, life was never that bad. Los Angeles, I'm tempted to say, wouldn't let it be. How could you take anything seriously in such a city? One night we stopped at what looked like a typical pizzeria, only to discover that it featured topless waitresses. Ours, a friendly, buxom housewife with two children, was delighted by Adrienne's pregnancy and urged her to buy a prescription ointment to prevent stretch marks. To prove its effectiveness, she leaned over the candle on the table, showing off her ample, unflawed breasts.

With free time on her hands, Adrienne sometimes sat in on my night course in Shakespearean tragedy at UCLA. She had performed in many of the plays, and we discussed them as we drove back and forth to the Westwood campus. She typed my class themes, typed a draft of a novel I was rewriting and typed my applications to grad school. Caught up in my preparations for the Graduate Record Exam, she coached me on general cultural knowledge, an area she excelled in, and we fell into a good-natured competition, with her quizzing me about artists, composers and architects and I challenging her on literary theory.

Every night before bed, she shampooed her hair and dried it in a ritual I liked to imagine she had witnessed growing up in the Far East. With the stylized choreography of Noh drama, she closed her eyes, cocked her hands on her hips and whipped her head back and forth. As long, dark tresses lashed at her face, she looked lost in a trance.

By her sixth month, her swollen breasts were marbled with faint blue veins and her navel, to my astonishment, had turned inside out. Red stretch marks had appeared on her hips and belly, and I took pleasure in rubbing the ointment the topless waitress had recommended onto the glazed swells of Adrienne's body.

What stuns me now—to be honest, it stunned me then—was that this didn't lead at once to new developments in our lovemaking. But

Adrienne had reservations about our having what she called "a fully realized relationship." She thought that sort of intimacy would leave us too dependent on one another and would cloud our judgment about the future. Sex, in her opinion, should be like icing on a cake. Before we treated ourselves to it, we needed to build a solid foundation, layer by layer.

One Saturday night as we lazed in bed, naked in each other's arms, kissing and caressing, I pressed close and, by sheer accident, found myself inside her. Jackknifing at the waist, she rolled away from me.

"You did it," she said. "You knew I didn't want to, but you went ahead and did it."

I almost denied it. I definitely did deny that I'd done it on purpose. "Anyway," I argued jesuitically, "it was so quick you really couldn't call it intercourse."

"Yes, it was," she insisted.

Swallowing an impulse to apologize for doing what couples in love and in bed usually did, I stalked off to sleep on the living room couch. Gazing up at the whitewashed ceiling, I wondered what, in these circumstances, a normal man would do. Just as it was becoming apparent that a normal man wouldn't be in these circumstances, Adrienne begged me to come back to bed. This time, there was no ambivalence about my intentions or hers, and her philosophy of slow baking combusted into flames.

We left town almost every weekend, driving to the desert or the mountains, to Palm Springs or Lake Arrowhead. After a bullfight in Tijuana, we traveled down the Baja Peninsula, untouristed at that time, and slept in the sand dunes. We caught the ferry to

Catalina and spent the night in a house that had belonged to Zane Grey. Trapped by an out-of-season snowstorm on the summit of Big Bear, we pretended to be snowbound like Lara and Dr. Zhivago.

Yet these joyriding getaways, which I recognized as attempts to blot out that weekend Adrienne had spent in New York, couldn't disguise the shadows on our lives. Isolated in an enormous city, afraid to make new friends, afraid of being found out by old friends, I was living with a woman I barely knew, a woman whose every mood and move I studied like cards. This was where I could have used the advice of my father, a gambler adept at figuring the odds, assuming a poker face and calculating when to hold them and when to fold them.

Adrienne, by contrast, may have felt that she was getting to know me all too well. My foul temper and volatility, my insecurities, suspicions and brooding. But she couldn't seem to quit inflaming them. It bothered me that she wrote bogus accounts of her life to her parents. Whatever we did together, she pretended to have done alone. Appropriating my job and the class at UCLA, she spoke of the progress she was making at work and in her personal interests. I suppose I should have taken vicarious pleasure in her preening, but I felt that I was being edited out.

What irritated me far more was the correspondence she kept up with various men. There was a Yale law student, an air force pilot in Homestead, Florida, and a clutch of political contacts in Washington, D.C. When I complained, she laughed off my jealousy. These were mere acquaintances, she said, boys she had dated casually, if at all.

Then one day, as I brought in the mail, I noticed a letter addressed to Adrienne in handwriting I hadn't seen before. On the back of the envelope, Dave's name and address looked like they had been scrawled by somebody who couldn't control the pen or his emotions. In spots, the ballpoint had punched tiny holes in the paper.

He had found her, and it wasn't hard to figure out how he had done it. Adrienne conceded right away that she had written him.

"Why?" I demanded. "I thought you were so worried about secrecy. I thought you were afraid of being followed. Now you practically send him a map."

"I needed to know his medical history—his blood type and so forth—for the adoption people."

"What adoption people? Have you contacted an agency?"

"Not yet. I was getting the information first and letting Dave know that I'm okay and Godot will be adopted by good parents."

"Are you okay?" I was shouting now. "You could have fooled me."

"Why are you so angry?"

"What do you expect? Looks to me like you're keeping your options open."

"That's not true. Here, read it." She shoved the open envelope into my hands. "Does it sound like a love letter?"

What Dave had written sounded as aggrieved and outraged as my voice, and it gave me my first inkling of what he was going through. He had been "hoping against hope," he wrote, that she'd change her mind and let him join her in LA. Now he knew there was no chance of that. Still, he pleaded with her. He had heard that couples were willing to shell out thousands of dollars for a healthy white child. If it was a question of money, he promised to pay Adrienne whatever she wanted if he could keep their baby.

She sank to her knees in front of me. "Is this the kind of apology you want? I'm sorry I wrote him. Should I prostrate myself? I'm sorry I'm pregnant, I'm sorry I'm alive." She wrapped her arms around my knees. I was reminded of the night when I had wrestled to keep her in the *Calvert Review* office. Now she was struggling to hold me. "I'm not too proud to beg. It would kill me if you left."

I crouched and took her in my arms. To my distress, I couldn't imagine leaving her, couldn't guess what it would take to force me to go.

"Help me, Mike. Don't keep finding fault," she said. "I already know I'm awful. What I don't know is how to go about giving up the baby. Can't you do it?"

S anta Ana winds blew all day, seething with heat and crackling with static electricity. Driving aimlessly through my sales territory, which encompassed telescopic distances of the San Fernando Valley, I tried to think. But it was difficult to concentrate with smoke and ash from wildfires swirling across my windshield. Something was wrong and had to be set right. Or was the wrong inside me? Was I too touchy and sensitive and, as Adrienne said, too stupidly jealous?

Now that Dave knew where she was, I worried what might unravel next. What if I had an accident and totaled the T-bird? Adrienne's parents would find out, and that would finish us. Or would it bring us closer together? Depending on my mood, the prospect of a crash was appealing or appalling.

I stopped in Reseda at an outdoor phone booth. The air was thick with grit and the booth hot as a griddle. I took off my coat and tie and returned to the air-conditioned car until I had things straight in my mind. Then I dialed the only adoption agency I had ever heard of, the Florence Crittenden Foundation.

"Are you interested in adopting, or do you have a baby to relinquish?" asked a chirpy receptionist, like a saleslady inquiring about some inconsequential matter of style or color.

"I'm calling for a friend," I said. "For information. She's pregnant."

The receptionist asked, How old was my friend? Was she married? Had she had previous children? How far along was she?

When I told her seven months, the receptionist exclaimed, "That's late. Most girls move in with us before they start to show."

"They live at the agency?"

"Yes, we're a residential institution. We provide counseling and medical care and arrangements for—"

"My friend has a place to live. She's happy there. What she wants is to make sure her baby winds up with a good family."

The receptionist explained that the Florence Crittenden Foundation didn't accept nonresidential clients. My friend would have to go elsewhere. She recommended the Children's Home Society of California.

I retreated to the cool, processed air of the car. Hiding from more than the heat and the wind that buzzed dust against the windshield like a dentist's drill, I was having as tough a time as Adrienne admitting that this was why we were here—not to play house together but to give away a baby.

When I got through to a caseworker at the Children's Home Society—I'll call her Mrs. Christian—she too voiced concern that we had waited so long. By this stage, Adrienne should have been seeing a doctor on a weekly basis. The agency accepted nonresidential clients, but it required girls to undergo a schedule of counseling sessions. If we delayed much longer, Mrs. Christian said, she might not be able to help us. She urged me to have my friend show up on Saturday for a preliminary meeting and a doctor's appointment.

"Now, what's her name?" Mrs. Christian asked.

Adrienne had used my name since coming to California, so I spelled out Mewshaw.

That Saturday, I planned to stay home and finish *King Lear*. But Adrienne pleaded that she'd be lonely without me. She'd get lost on the freeway. She'd feel lost with Mrs. Christian. Well aware of sounding like a hapless waif, she hammed it up, pulling her face into a mask of comic melancholy until I agreed to keep her company.

During the drive, she smoked, fidgeted and said little. Lighting a cigarette, she took a single puff, complained that it tasted terrible and threw it out the window. "What should we tell this woman?" she said. "She's bound to ask questions about you."

"Why not tell her the truth?"

"I don't know. It's bad enough that I'm unmarried and pregnant and giving up a baby. What'll she think if she learns we're living together?"

"She'll take it in stride. She deals with stranger situations every day."

"She doesn't deal with me every day. My private life is none of her business. Can't we say you're my brother?"

I had no compunction about lying to protect Adrienne, but this struck me as silly. "She'll never believe that," I said.

"Why not? We look enough alike to be related. And what does it matter whether she believes me? At least I won't have to discuss our relationship."

I said it was up to her; I didn't care. But of all the things I might have been to Adrienne, why would she pass me off as her brother? And what was it about our relationship that made her reluctant to talk about it?

Off the freeway, we entered an area of small cinder-block homes and the occasional large wooden house that had been subdivided into rental units, bail bondsmen's offices and storefront churches. Lined with palm trees, spangled with bougainvillea and geraniums, the streets had the somnolent, semitropical feel of the Caribbean. Black people thronged every park bench, porch and bus stop. They didn't look unhappy or menacing, as the population of an urban ghetto in the East might have. But in the next year these streets would explode with race riots. Molotov cocktails would touch off fires, and dozens would die.

The Children's Home Society occupied the neighborhood's biggest and best-preserved building. Gingerbread Gothic in decor, it had the incongruous appearance of a wedding cake. All it lacked was a miniature candy couple on top. But I didn't think of this irony as I pulled up the gravel drive. I thought of Adrienne's grandmother's farmhouse, white frame and formidable, yet cheek by jowl with a junkyard. Outside the front gate here, everybody was black and poor. Inside, everyone—doctors, nurses, caseworkers and clients—was white.

Neither Adrienne nor I knew anything about the Children's Home Society. We knew nothing about any adoption agency. Less research had gone into this than into our weekend excursions. But we had lucked into a good thing. Established in 1872 as a nonprofit organization for orphans and foundlings, CHS had offices throughout the state and had handled over forty thousand adoptions. In 1964 alone, it would place twelve hundred children with adoptive parents.

Mrs. Christian, a middle-aged woman in a shirtwaist dress, led us upstairs to her office. On its window ledges perched a collection of dolls in international costumes. Mrs. Christian told us she bought a new doll every time she traveled, and judging by their number, she traveled a lot.

Once we were seated, she said, "Now, you're Adrienne Mewshaw. I remember that much." Turning to me, she added, "But I don't believe I caught your name."

"Michael Mewshaw."

Smiling, Mrs. Christian nodded. It was impossible to read anything except pleasant attentiveness on her face. "Since you've waited this long, I suppose you two have discussed your decision."

She paused for a response, and when none was forthcoming, she said, "These sessions are very important to us. We like to get to know each girl personally. And of course their husbands and boyfriends when possible."

"Maybe you already told my brother," Adrienne said, "but could you explain how you place babies?"

Mrs. Christian glanced at me, jotted something in a notepad, then shifted her gaze to Adrienne. Prospective parents, she said, underwent interviews and counseling sessions, just as the girls did. Since CHS did its best to match adoptees with families of the same race, religion and cultural background, anything Adrienne was willing to share about herself and the birth father would assist in the placement.

Once again, Mrs. Christian paused for a reaction. Once again, Adrienne offered none. She stared over her stomach, into her lap.

"For most girls," Mrs. Christian continued, "this is a time of great emotional turmoil. We understand that and have to be sure they're making an informed decision of their own free will. Because once the papers are signed . . ."

She didn't finish. She didn't need to. In those days, all parties to an adoption understood that the process was irrevocable. With a new birth certificate in his or her adopted name, the child would have no way of tracing its biological parents, and the birth parents would be in the same fix, with no way of finding their child.

I asked Mrs. Christian to leave Adrienne and me alone for a few minutes. Seemingly well acquainted with unexpected requests, she said, "Of course," and stepped out of the office.

"I think you should level with her," I told Adrienne.

"Why?"

"She explained why. It'll help them place the baby and help you get something out of these sessions."

"Like what?" She still had her head down, her eyes fixed on her lap.

"Like understanding why you're so upset."

"I don't need her to understand that."

"Maybe she can help you deal with it."

She looked up at me, her one lazy eye slightly unfocused. "Are you sure you're not the one who's upset?"

"Look, Adrienne, we've both got a lot ahead of us in the next two months. This seems like the best place to start."

She laid her hand in the crook of my arm, rubbing the fabric of my shirt between her fingertips. "Will you do the talking?"

"I will at first. Then it's up to you."

When Mrs. Christian came back, I told her I wasn't Adrienne's brother and I wasn't the baby's father. But I loved her, and I was living with her and hoped to marry her.

She assimilated this news with bland professional calm, thanked me for my candor and asked to speak to Adrienne in private. A moment later I was out in the lobby attempting to read *King Lear*. I kept losing track of Shakespeare as I replayed the conversation with Mrs. Christian. I didn't want to believe that secrets were all that bound Adrienne and me together. Still, it was unsettling to have her behind a closed door discussing things with a stranger.

It would have helped if I had had someone to talk to. Ideally, I should have sought counseling rather than simply urge it on Adrienne. There was so much I didn't understand. But in that era, when, as the novelist Dan Chaon has put it, adoption "was a machine for misery" and the assumption was that only promiscuous or improvident people fell into the predicament, advice, much less sympathy, was in short supply. Women went through it alone, and even men willing to be involved were isolated.

It was as if each new out-of-wedlock pregnancy were unprecedented, and although millions of illegitimate babies had been born, no information could be shared for fear that it would encourage bad behavior. Examples of strength, sources of consolation, existed all around yet remained achingly out of reach.

Several short blocks west of our apartment on North Harper, the low-rent district gave way to an enclave of palatial mansions. In one of them lived Loretta Young, the movie star and television personality. I saw her every Sunday at St. Victor's Catholic Church. She arrived in a Rolls-Royce and strolled into mass, regal and serene.

Decades later I would read that as a twenty-two-year-old ingenue, Loretta Young had had an illegitimate daughter with Clark Gable. To save his career and hers, she disappeared and left the baby in an orphanage in San Francisco. By the time the little girl turned two, Young had married, and she and her husband adopted the child.

I wish I had known that and had had a chance to talk to her. I wish I could have spoken to anyone. Instead, I stumbled along as best I could, while behind closed doors, Adrienne did the same.

Fortunately, she came to trust and like Mrs. Christian. She liked the obstetrician at CHS too. It pleased her that he had adopted children of his own. But he threw her into a quandary when he said that he'd like to adopt Adrienne's baby. In the end, she refused. She couldn't bear to know who was raising her baby. She didn't want to be tempted to reconnect with the child. That the child might try to reconnect with her was something that never occurred to us.

CHAPTER ELEVEN

A few weeks after Lyndon Johnson won the presidential election in a landslide over Barry Goldwater, the balmy fall weather broke and a cold rain fell for days, soaking the city and bleeding grease over the freeways. Gutters overflowed, washing the sidewalks ankle deep in water. Then the water ominously clouded with silt, and mudslides buried backyards and automobiles. Hillside houses, no longer able to hold on to their foundations, plunged down into canyons, trailing pipes and electrical wires. Swimming pools skidded down the same tracks, scattering blue shells like giant robin's eggs.

The sun didn't reappear until after Thanksgiving, a month before the baby was due. At the office, I got a message from Mrs. Christian, saying to phone her ASAP. Worried that Adrienne had gone into labor prematurely, I called and asked, "What's wrong?"

"Nothing. I just thought it was time you and I had a chat."

I said I'd be at the agency, as usual, on Saturday. But she preferred to talk now.

"Let me change phones," I said, eager to escape Friden's open-plan office where other salesmen milled about.

"It'd be better if we did this in person. Are you free to come here?"

Webbed with grillwork, Mrs. Christian's windows let in afternoon light, laying what appeared to be prison bars on the opposing walls. Outside, gardeners in gray uniforms were mowing the lawn. Unlike the dolls in their international costumes, Mrs. Christian was dressed in a nondescript skirt and blouse and wore no makeup. She said that Adrienne had told her a lot about me, but she wanted to get to know me herself. It had also occurred to her that I might have questions.

Wasting an opportunity to confide what I was feeling, I denied that I had any questions. But Mrs. Christian had plenty of her own. How was my job? My night course? My writing? My graduate school applications?

Then she took a sudden tangent from these polite inquiries. "Was Adrienne pregnant when you two started dating?" It was what Amy would ask decades later.

"No," I said.

"Then how can you be sure the baby's not yours?"

"Ask Adrienne."

"I have. She says you're not the father."

"I told you that the day we met."

"The Children's Home Society has to be positive. We've had cases where girls relinquish babies, and later on the birth father makes trouble. You can imagine the legal mess."

"Does Adrienne have to have the father's permission?"

"Not normally. But this isn't a normal case, and we need to have all the facts."

"Well, the fact is that Adrienne and I didn't have intercourse until she was five months pregnant."

"I see." From a desk drawer, she removed a manila folder.

"Hasn't she told you this?" I asked.

"I'm afraid I can't discuss our conferences. They're confidential. I'd appreciate it if you'd sign a release swearing you're not the father and have no claim."

"No claim to what?"

"To the baby. It's to complete our records. No one'll ever see it. After the adoption, the file is sealed."

"Then what's the point? Why sign something nobody'll see?"

"It's to protect Adrienne and the adoptive parents."

"And to protect the Children's Home Society?" I guessed.

"Yes, that too. But let's not make this into something it's not. The statement will protect you as well."

"I don't need protection."

"There's no reason to get upset, Mike. The release just repeats the facts as you've stated them."

Maybe she was right; I had no reason to be upset. But I can't deny that I was. "Look," I said, "is this CHS policy, or did Adrienne push for a release?"

"I've explained that I can't discuss what Adrienne might or might not have said. She's my client, and my first responsibility is to her. But in general terms, I can say that she's anxious about things."

"Anxious that I'll claim the baby's mine?"

"You're asking again for specifics. Let's just leave it that she's anxious about the future."

"So am I," I conceded.

"That's natural," she said in a soothing voice. "What do you expect afterward?"

I knew better than to ask whether the question came from Adrienne. Mrs. Christian would only repeat that she couldn't tell me. Tired of trying to tease out what she had in mind, I decided to admit what I had in mine. "I love Adrienne." Somehow this sounded truculent, so in a softer tone I added, "After the baby's born, I hope we'll get married."

Mrs. Christian was fiddling with a pencil, fingering the eraser, then testing the graphite point. "That's one of the things Adrienne's anxious about. Without going into details, she feels a lot of family pressure. And she's aware what a serious matter marriage would be for you as a Catholic. She's concerned about, you know, differences in attitudes toward divorce, birth control, child rearing."

"I wish she had told me. We could work it out."

"Yes, when the time's right, you two need to talk."

She was still fidgeting with the pencil. I couldn't help asking, "Doesn't she want to marry me?"

"That's not for me to say, Mike."

I followed up with a question that even today makes me cringe. "Doesn't she love me?"

"I know she has very strong feelings for you. She cares about you. But right now, with all that's going on for Adrienne, I don't think you should count on anything."

As the weight of what she said sank in, it had the paradoxical effect of making me feel light-headed. It lifted me to my feet.

"Where are you going?" Mrs. Christian asked.

I didn't know. I just wanted to get away.

"Please, sit down," she said.

I did as instructed.

"I shouldn't have said don't count on anything. You should count on yourself. Finish college. Go to grad school. Make your own decisions, and let Adrienne make hers."

I felt too deflated to speak.

"I wish you'd talk to me, Mike. Or if my being Adrienne's case-worker makes you uncomfortable, I'll find another counselor."

Here was my chance again—an opportunity to open up. But I couldn't do it.

Filling the silence, Mrs. Christian covered the same ground, going back over the importance of my signing a release, just as the gardeners outside went back and forth across the lawn. When I refused to do what she asked, she returned the manila folder to the drawer and said, "I don't want you to leave until you promise not to mention any of this to Adrienne. By coming to California, you made a commitment to her, and I think you should honor it."

I didn't have the presence of mind to ask whether Adrienne hadn't made a commitment to me.

"I'm worried about you, Mike. I'm worried about Adrienne too. If anything goes wrong in these last weeks, I know you'll never forgive yourself. For everybody's sake, let's agree to keep this between us."

As I left the Children's Home Society, a din of questions replaced the drone of the power mowers. Had my ignorance and immaturity, my jealousy and anger, destroyed what I might have had with Adrienne? Would a different man, a better man, have made her happy? Or had she known from the start what she meant to do?

Now, in addition to the lies I told my family and the people at work, not to mention the lies I told myself, I began to live on false terms with Adrienne. Clamming up about Mrs. Christian, I floated in an ether of dishonesty and reversed all my instinctive responses, whispering when I wanted to scream, declaring undying love when I felt dead.

In this disorienting fog, it was hardly surprising that one afternoon when I parked in the Friden lot, I forgot to set the hand brake on the T-bird. As I stepped into the building, I heard the screech of metal on metal. Adrienne's car would have rolled into the maelstrom of rush-hour traffic on Beverly Boulevard had it not sideswiped a Friden van and snagged on its bumper. Days later, driving a car lent by the repair shop, I had a fender bender. If anybody ever seemed destined for a crack-up, I was that man.

Right before Christmas, Adrienne received a card and a check for $500 from her parents. That was a sizable sum of money in 1964— as much as I earned in a month. She didn't deposit it in our joint bank account, and I didn't ask her to. Instead, as if vying with the Dalys for their daughter's love, I withdrew every dollar we didn't need to save for the doctor and set out on a spending spree. At I. Magnin's I bought Adrienne a silk blouse, a nightgown trimmed with Belgian lace to wear in the hospital and a pair of suede slacks for when she had her figure back.

Early on the morning of December 24, she went into labor. With traffic heavy on the Harbor Freeway, we wasted a tense half-hour easing toward our exit and were delayed again by an accident a block away from California Lutheran Hospital. A Fuller Brush salesman had plowed into a parked car, littering South Hope Street with combs, mops and bottles of cleanser.

In that era before a husband's hands-on participation in the delivery room became almost mandatory, a woman was whisked away to be prepped for childbirth while the man completed the paperwork. A red-headed nurse, her face spangled with freckles, rolled a registration form into a manual typewriter and rapped out questions at me. When she asked what kind of health insurance we carried and I said none, her fingers paused over the keys and her tone of voice changed. "How will you be paying? Credit card?"

"No."

"Personal checks have to be preapproved," she cautioned me.

"We've made other arrangements," I said.

"Is this a charity case?"

"No. I'm supposed to pay the Children's Home Society."

"So it's an agency case?"

"I guess that's what you call it."

"Why didn't you say so?" Giving me a withering glare, she ripped the form from the typewriter and tossed it into a trash basket. "You can go to the waiting room."

For the next eleven hours, I paced the floor and fretted, to all appearances an archetypical expectant father. As company, I had a black boy of about fourteen, his hair in an Afro as puffed up and bristly as a porcupine. Unlike me, he displayed nerveless cool. When a nurse told him he had a new baby brother, the kid bopped off to the nursery, abandoning me to my worries.

For all my concern about Adrienne, I found myself obsessing about the baby. Until then, Godot had been a disembodied force that had brought Adrienne and me together and might drive us apart. This was the first time I had thought of it as a person, a human being, and it filled me with anguish to imagine what might befall it. If it was born with birth defects, nobody would adopt it. Even if healthy, it would be brought up by strangers. I needed no reminders that adoptions didn't always pan out. From living with Lee, my foster brother, I knew that anything—violence, sexual abuse, even murder—was possible.

When Adrienne had told me she was pregnant, I had assumed that any life was better than no life. Now, I wasn't so sure. Having seen the nurse's glare, I prayed that her contempt stopped with me and didn't extend to the baby.

At 6:36 P.M., a different nurse darted into the waiting room, her rubber-soled shoes squeaking. "Congratulations, Mr. Mewshaw; you have a daughter. A big one. Eight pounds and fourteen ounces. The mother will be a little sore for a few days, but she's doing fine, and you can see her in a jiffy. First, I bet you'd like to meet your little girl."

I wasn't convinced I was supposed to see her. Adoption lore had it that illegitimate babies vanished from the hospital before a parent could lay eyes on them. This wrenching separation was said to be less painful. But I didn't believe that and refused to miss my chance.

Near the nursery, in an adjoining room, an orderly with a cotton mask over his nose and mouth wheeled in a clear plastic crib. In block letters, it was labeled GIRL MEWSHAW. The nurse reached into the crib and removed the baby's diaper. Her hands looked crude and rough next to the smooth-skinned infant. She rolled her this way and that to show me that the tiny girl was perfect. "Beautiful, isn't she?" the nurse asked.

I agreed and smoothed Godot's damp, dark hair. I wanted to pick her up but feared that I wouldn't be able to bring myself to put her down again. Gesturing to the safety pin that glinted in the bud of the baby's navel, I asked whether that was necessary. The nurse assured me that it was.

As the orderly wheeled the crib away, Godot was crying and beating her fists at the air.

"Now, if you'll sign this . . ." The nurse held out a clipboard, indicating the space on a form next to FATHER.

"I'm not the father," I said.

"You're not Mr. Mewshaw?" she asked, perplexed.

"Yes, but I'm not the father."

"If you're a relative, you can pinch hit."

"I'm not related." To put us both out of our shriveling misery, I explained, "It's an agency case."

Her lips pursed into a small, silent O. Then she said, "You can see your . . . the mother's over here."

I followed her through a pair of swinging doors, down a hall to a dim room where Adrienne was in a bed against the far wall. Her body, slim again, barely wrinkled the sheet. I noticed that her teeth had worn a groove in her lower lip where she had bitten down during the long labor. She was crying but said it was in joy, not sadness. "Isn't Godot lovely? She looks just like my mother."

When I leaned over to kiss her, she hugged my head to her breast. "I'm so happy."

A fter Christmas mass at St. Victor's with Loretta Young, I returned to California Lutheran Hospital for visiting hours, suffused with a rare sense of well-being. I hadn't forgotten what Mrs. Christian had warned me, but I felt hopeful and believed there was reason to suspect that she had been wrong. Adrienne treated me with a sort of urgent tenderness, and whenever I was slow to touch her, she took my hand and laid it where she wanted it, on her breast.

The next night I brought her eggnog, spiked with bourbon. It was no problem smuggling it past the nurses' station. Sharing a toothbrush glass, we drank toasts to the baby, to each other, then to the waning days of 1964 and the advent of 1965.

The morning she was released from the hospital, Adrienne walked with me to the nursery window. I still wasn't convinced that we were allowed to do this, but no one stopped us. With tears in her eyes, she tapped the glass as she might tap the side of an aquarium and whispered, "Bye-bye, Godot."

CHAPTER TWELVE

To people at work, I lied that the baby suffered serious respiratory ailments and had to remain in the hospital, in intensive care. No one was permitted to visit her. Shortly after New Year's, I submitted my resignation at Friden, informing them that I was going back to college.

Apart from packing, this left one piece of unfinished business. Adrienne had to return to the Children's Home Society to sign the final relinquishment papers. As always, she asked me to accompany her, and while I was there, Mrs. Christian again urged me to sign a release. It seemed stupid and stubborn not to. On a plain sheet of stationery I scribbled a single line: "I, Michael F. Mewshaw, am not the father of the baby born to Adrienne Daly on December 24, 1964." I dated the document January 12, 1965.

Then, on a cool, overcast morning, we stowed our accumulated belongings in the Thunderbird and struck out for Maryland. Along with the baby, we left behind a forwarding address care of a post box in Bowie, not far from the university. Both of us dreaded the final doctor's bill being delivered to our parents' house.

As we crossed the LA city limits, Adrienne sighed that she felt relieved to be heading east. I was ambivalent. While the life we had cobbled together for the last five months had been based on lies and had never been less than fraught, I thought we had accomplished something to be proud of. But by the end of the month, I'd be trapped at home, hitchhiking back and forth to school and scratching for money to see Adrienne on weekends. Presuming I had time to see her. If I cared to graduate in June, I had to pass seven courses in the spring semester.

Adrienne didn't chime in with her familiar cheerful encouragement. She didn't say, "As long as I have a car, you'll always have a ride. And now that I can work, you won't be short of money." Nor was there any hint that we might rent a student apartment together.

Instead, she mused that she too faced rough months ahead. She needed to rebuild bridges with her family. Her parents would expect her to live at home, and she worried that her milk wouldn't dry up and her stretch marks wouldn't fade, and her mother would notice them. Her grandmother was in Florida for the winter, and it pained Adrienne that she hadn't seen her favorite relative for so long. Maybe she'd have to make a short visit.

I listened, said little and struggled to keep a lid on my emotions. I longed to believe that she wouldn't have discussed her plans if the life she described didn't include me.

In no hurry to get where we were going, I meandered along secondary roads, through Indian reservations in Arizona and ghost towns and deserted mining claims in New Mexico. A foot of snow covered the ground in Santa Fe, so we veered south for warmth, and as we approached Albuquerque, I mentioned that my father lived there. Adrienne said she'd like to meet him.

In my whole life I had never before acknowledged to anyone that I had a father in Albuquerque, and it never would have occurred to me to introduce a friend, much less someone I loved, to the man who shared a name but little else with me. But suddenly it hit me how foolish I had been. By denying my father's existence, I belittled my own identity. What was there to be ashamed of? I couldn't let my mother's twisted preoccupation with secrecy distort my life.

On a different level, less complicated, though no less powerful, I longed to show up on his doorstep in a T-bird with a beautiful woman. Last August when I had been en route to LA, he had made me feel like a fool, and I had left thinking that he believed I would never amount to anything. Here was a chance to change that.

He and his wife, Blanche, insisted we spend the night in their small, mock-adobe cottage. Adrienne and I told them that we had met through mutual friends in LA and when we realized we were both bound for Maryland we agreed to split the driving and expenses. I was put up in a bedroom with my half-brother Dennis, and Adrienne shared a bed with my eight-year-old half-sister Robyn. After dinner, while Adrienne paired off with Blanche in the kitchen, I stayed in the living room with my father, bragging about my success at Friden. I showed him the gold tie clasp, embossed with a miniature desktop computer, that I had won as salesman of the month. I said I'd like him to have it as a belated Christmas present.

He accepted it with thanks but allowed as how he didn't know when he'd ever wear it. Mostly he wore open-collar sport shirts or a string tie and bolo on dress-up occasions. Lifting his chin toward the sound of Adrienne's voice, he asked, "Where's she live?"

"Bethesda."

An ex–cab driver, he remembered the Washington area well. "Nice address. Her family must be loaded. She's not for you, Mike."

I nearly exploded. Why would he assume I wasn't good enough? Why didn't I deserve a woman like Adrienne? I was tempted to shake him by the shoulders and shout that she loved me, had lived with me and depended on me all during her pregnancy. Instead, I mumbled my deepest fear: "I'll probably never see her again once we get to the East Coast."

"Good," he said. "She's not your type. What are you doing next year?"

"Grad school."

"How are you going to pay for it?"

"A grant."

"And if you don't win one?"

I shrugged. "I'll join the Peace Corps."

"Forget that crap, Mike. Grad school, the Peace Corps, that's not for people like you. That's for fancy girls from Bethesda and guys born rich. Join the army, get your military obligation out of the way and find a steady job."

Next morning, when Adrienne and I set off after breakfast, the Friden tie clasp still lay on an end table beside my father's chair. For the rest of the day, as we headed south, Adrienne's questions came down on me like the snow squalls that pelted the mountains. She said she liked Blanche but wished she had gotten a clearer fix on my father. I didn't mention that I had no fix on him at all. She asked about his background, why he had never gone to college, why he and my mother had broken up, where Blanche came from, whether she had graduated from college.

Her interest in my family's past annoyed me almost as much as my father's disparagement of my future. Both seemed freighted with contempt and the implication that I was going nowhere. As if to prove them all wrong, I proposed that we take a side trip, a detour from the trek home. I was eager to show Adrienne another part of Mexico and a crucial aspect of myself.

Parking the T-bird on a pay lot in El Paso, we boarded an overnight bus that stank of diesel fumes, live poultry and dead air. For a woman who had had a baby three weeks ago, Adrienne was a hardy traveler, as stoical as any Indian we passed along the roadside. She never complained about the crowds, the bus stations with open latrines or the swarming whores who stroked her lustrous hair and crooned, "*¡Qué guapa!*"

At dawn in Durango, as we drank *café con leche* while waiting to change buses for Mazatlán, two American college boys overheard us speaking English. They said they were headed for the Pacific coast too, and they offered to make room in their VW convertible and let us ride along. We spent a week carousing with these strangers, drinking tequila and body surfing at deserted beaches. Quickly sniffing out that we might not be quite as married as we claimed to be, both fellows had their eyes on Adrienne, but for me this only added an exciting subtext.

From Mazatlán we beetled north to Los Mochis, where the college boys fell in with a couple of coeds from Arizona State and Adrienne and I met a one-eyed pilot who promised to fly us to Nogales, Arizona, if we didn't mind strapping ourselves into the jump seats of his crop duster. After that and another overnight bus ride to El Paso, we retrieved the T-bird and pushed east.

Adrienne declared that she had never had so much fun. I told her that this was how I planned to spend my life—hopscotching around the globe, visiting places I had read about and wanted to write about. Since she had grown up all over the world and agreed that we made great traveling companions, why didn't we stick together?

She paused. She paused so long that her silence became embarrassing. "Let's wait," she finally said, "and see how things work out in the next few years."

"What am I—on trial? Don't the months we just spent together count for something?"

"Of course they do. But like you said a few days ago, we have some hard choices ahead of us."

To me, the most important one was whether to get married. But Adrienne enumerated the many uncertainties I faced. I had to finish my BA. Then I had to hope I would win a grant and decide where I'd go to grad school. "Doesn't it make more sense," she said, "to focus on that rather than discuss marriage now?"

"We already discussed it. Remember last spring? You said you were just marking time until we got married this summer."

"A lot has happened since then."

"Yeah, a hell of a lot. But I don't see how that changes the main thing. If anything, we're closer now."

"You'd actually want to be married while you're still in school?"

"I was in school this fall, and we did fine living together as man and wife."

"That's not the same, Mike. And it's not the point."

"What is the point?"

"It's just, I don't know, I need time to think."

"Texas is a big state," I told her. "By the time we reach Dallas, I'd like an answer. Do you want to marry me or not?"

We made it as far as the Monahans Sand Dunes before she spoke. "Okay, I want to marry you."

"When?"

"The question was *whether.*"

"You answered that. Now it's *when*."

"Why are you doing this to me?" she wailed as though it were torture to talk about a wedding date.

This time the silence lasted many hours, through Odessa and Midland, through a dinner of chicken-fried steak and into a Ramada Inn. Adrienne had no clean nightclothes and borrowed a T-shirt from me to sleep in. She slid under the covers of one double bed. I climbed into the other. After I switched off the lamp, she moved over to my bed, curling against me spoon fashion, her back against my chest. I held her as I used to when she was pregnant, one hand on her breasts, the other on her belly. But I said nothing and did nothing.

The next day, I announced that I was flying to Washington from Dallas. Following the signs to Love Field, I sped over the sere winter plains to a terminal that I, like most Americans at that time, remembered from when John F. Kennedy's casket was loaded aboard a plane bound for Andrews Air Force Base. Nudging the transmission into park, leaving the engine running, I said, "I guess this is it."

"I can't believe you're being so pigheaded."

I got out, popped the trunk, grabbed my sea bag and walked away. At the Braniff counter I had been in line a few minutes when Adrienne appeared, quietly sobbing. "Don't do this," she said.

"Why should I stay? So you can leave me once we're in Maryland?"

"I'll marry you," she said, choking back tears.

"It's obvious that's not what you want. It's been obvious for a long time."

"I mean it," she said. "I'll call my parents and tell them we're engaged."

Pulling me out of line to a phone booth, she placed a collect call and broke the news to her mother in a voice whose manifest falseness reminded me of a woman with a gun at her head attempting to send a distress signal. It made me heartsick to hear hollow phrases that I wished were true.

After she hung up, I said that since I was at the airport, I might as well catch a flight to Washington. It would give us both time to think. Adrienne didn't disagree. She kissed me good-bye and promised to call as soon as she got to D.C.

T

rue to her word, Adrienne phoned from the road and we ren-
dezvoused at the Key Bridge Marriott Hotel, across the Po-
tomac River from Georgetown. It would be the last night we ever slept
together. In the morning, she drove to her family's home, and I caught
a cab to mine. We didn't see one another again until the following
weekend, when I arrived in Bethesda to be introduced to the Dalys as
their daughter's fiancé.

They greeted me and the news of our engagement with chilly polite-
ness. Since I didn't have the money to buy Adrienne a ring, Mrs. Daly was
of the opinion that it was inappropriate to issue any public announcement.
Her parents were old-fashioned sticklers for formality, Adrienne explained.

Mr. Daly, a pale, soft version of John Wayne, scowled at me through
horn-rimmed glasses. He suffered from gout and carried a cane.

Mrs. Daly, a full-figured, frostily attractive woman, smoked cigarettes
in a plastic holder. She cleaned the holder with a Kleenex after each cig-

arette and showed me the nicotine residue, shaking her head in distaste as if this were the result of some nasty habit of mine. When she learned that I wrote, she professed a lively interest in literature and recounted how she had led a campaign to ban *Lady Chatterley's Lover* and *The Tropic of Cancer.* Although the Supreme Court had ruled that such bans violated the First Amendment to the Constitution, Mrs. Daly remained unrepentant. She detested most modern novelists, especially a vile, immoral Frenchman named Prew. Adrienne timidly interrupted to inform her mother that the "s" and "t" in "Proust" weren't silent.

Once the spring semester started, Adrienne and I were reduced to keeping in touch by telephone and huddling for an hour or two in campus hangouts where we had first dated. After the intimacy of our lives in LA, this was painful and frustrating. At least, it was for me.

Adrienne was more difficult to read. She continued to dwell on the need for secrecy. Scheduling a postnatal checkup at a distant clinic, she begged me to come with her but acted uncomfortable in my presence and kept glancing over her shoulder as if she feared we were being followed. It seemed a replay of last spring, when Dave had trailed us everywhere. Now it was her parents we had to be worried about. Adrienne warned me that if we spent too much time alone, the Dalys were liable to guess that we had lived together. Then they might guess why. But I suspected that she was determined to hide me along with what had happened in LA.

When I called, Mrs. Daly often claimed that Adrienne was out and forgot to pass on messages. Once when I stopped by to pick her up for dinner, Mrs. Daly swore that she had left for the evening. Just as she was shutting the door on me, Adrienne stepped out of her bedroom, and Mrs. Daly arched her eyebrows as if to say no sensible person could blame her for shielding her daughter from the likes of me.

I lost my temper and told Adrienne that I refused to be treated like as trespasser. She replied that her parents treated me no differently than they had every boy she had dated.

"I'm not *every* boy," I protested. "And we're not dating. We're supposed to be getting married. We're supposed to be in love."

As a novelist, I admire narrative shape and concision, and I wish there were some way of dramatizing how our relationship fell apart without replaying an ugly mess of arguments and accusations and horrific behavior on my part. I wish I had handled things better. I wish I had acquiesced to the end with grace. But I didn't. Deeply hurt at losing Adrienne, I hit back. I let her have it with both barrels. While she possessed the subtle skills of a bureaucratic infighter, I was a barroom brawler. I didn't care about scoring points. I wanted to win with a knockout.

"Why are you doing this?" Adrienne asked over and over. "Why are you destroying all the wonderful memories I have?"

I told her I didn't give a damn about memories or her good opinion of me if we were breaking up. How did she think I felt to have her dump me a month after the baby's birth? My mistake had been believing that she wouldn't jettison me as she had Dave.

These words flew back in my face. They proved, Adrienne argued, that bitterness had poisoned me. I'd never forgive her for getting pregnant, and never trust her again.

"Give me a reason to trust you," I said. "Stay and work this out."

She swore that she loved me but maintained that love wasn't enough. She had to get away and clear her head. In February, she flew to Florida, joining her grandmother at her winter home in Coral Gables.

After a week, Adrienne sent a letter. It didn't matter what she wrote. I was persuaded that we weren't finished as long as we were linked by a rosary of words. I wrote back pages and pages, an endless spill of feelings. She answered, and we started talking long distance. This too filled me with hope—until I listened to what she was saying. Her grandmother was taking her on an around-the-world tour that would last six months.

I stopped writing. I stopped calling.

One afternoon late that spring, as I walked down sorority row, I noticed a metallic-gray Thunderbird. I circled it twice to make sure it was Adrienne's and to give myself a chance to do the sane thing and keep going. Instead, I stopped at her sorority house, pasted on a smile for the housemother's benefit and explained that Adrienne Daly was here visiting friends and I wanted to surprise her. Could the housemother summon her to the reception area without mentioning my name?

While I waited, I felt a great shifting inside me, like ballast breaking free on a ship. It was time for drastic action. I had to heave this dangerous burden overboard and think of a healing gesture. Or a terminally hurtful one.

Smiling and self-possessed, Adrienne swanned into the room, betraying the mildest delight at seeing me. "Hello," she sang out and offered a hand for me to shake. I didn't take it. I didn't dare touch her until I decided what to do.

"Thought you were traveling with your grandmother," I said.

"We leave at the end of the week. I dropped in to say good-bye to the girls."

"That's nice. Look, you and I need to talk."

"Not now." Though she smiled, there was iron in her voice. Tanned from her time in Florida, as sleek as she had been when I met her little more than a year ago, she wore a clinging white knit dress with red piping at the collar. "Call me at home," she said.

"And have your mother hang up on me? No, thanks."

Three sorority sisters passed by, calling out to Adrienne, "Have fun on your trip. Send postcards."

"Thanks. You can count on it." Then to me, "I have lots of errands to run and packing to finish. What's there to talk about that we haven't said before?"

"Maybe there are things I'd like to say again. Maybe there are things you never heard."

"Let's go outside," she said.

I felt powerless in the grasp of an obsession that might drag me in any direction. Mayhem. Abject begging. Murder. A declaration of undying love.

For her part, Adrienne appeared to be torn between a desire to get away *from* me and a desire to get away *with* me to a place where no one would witness the foolishness she feared I was capable of. She handed me the car keys, as had been her habit in California, where I had done all the driving. I let her in and slid behind the wheel. Perhaps she expected us to sit there in the T-bird and talk—a sober scene to bookend the one in the Fiat when she had told me she was pregnant. But I revved the engine and roared out onto US1.

"Where are you going?"

"Wait and see."

"You said you wanted to talk. Stop and tell me what's on your mind."

"That's the last thing you'd like to hear—what's on my mind." It was also the last thing I'd be able to articulate.

"This isn't funny, Mike."

"It's not supposed to be funny. I've decided we should drive up to Havre de Grace and get married."

"Do I have a say in the matter?" She tried sarcasm.

"No, you don't."

"What are you, some Sicilian peasant kidnapping a girl to force her to marry? Even by your standards, this is ridiculous."

It sounded ridiculous to me too, but I didn't like hearing her say it. I liked it even less when she called me "pathetic." That was when I hit her. Not with words, as I had in the past. My hand flew off the steering wheel and clipped the bridge of her nose. Groaning, she buried her face in her hands. I pulled to the curb and pried her hands apart. Seeing no blood, no bruises or broken bones, I sped off before she could scramble out the door.

"If you don't let me out, I'll jump."

I ran a red light and rocketed through an intersection. She didn't threaten to jump again.

"Why are you doing this?" Adrienne screamed.

"I love you."

"You love me and you hit me? That's crazy."

It didn't sound rational to me either. Even in the moment, I realized I was comporting myself like a lunatic. Or part of me did. Another part felt that she was the crazy one and had pushed me to this. When I told Adrienne that I felt betrayed and doubted that she had ever been honest about anything, she said, "Listen to yourself. You're not making sense. You say you love me. You say we should get married. But you talk like I'm the worst person in the world."

Soaring around a cloverleaf, I swung onto the Beltway, setting the car loose like a canoe on a river current, circling the DC suburbs for hours. Adrienne continued talking, pointing out inconsistencies in everything I said. I listened to her, just as she had challenged me to listen to myself. The drive, the conversation, devolved into a repetitive, long-playing record. I didn't like what I heard and didn't care for the person saying it. She was right, although not in the way she intended. This didn't make sense. Why should I love her, much less want to be with her, after what she had done?

Finally I swung the T-bird around, and we returned to the university in the dark. From Adrienne's sorority house, where I parked, it was a short walk to the spot where I started hitchhiking home.

. . .

That should have been it. The end with an exclamation point. Adrienne would have been within her rights to have me arrested and jailed for kidnapping and assault. Recognizing how close to the brink I had teetered, I wanted no more of that. But Adrienne, as always, remained a confounding enigma. At the airport, the day of her departure for the around-the-world trip, she took out a six-figure insurance policy and named me the beneficiary. She wrote a long letter, tumbling with emotion, from Vietnam. Then she sent a shorter one from India, along with a copy of her itinerary, listing hotel addresses and phone numbers where I could contact her.

I never replied.

By the time she returned, almost eight months later, I was in graduate school at the University of Virginia. Over the Christmas holidays, close to the baby's birthday, we bumped into each other at a wedding in Washington. We had dinner together, and afterward—I hope this doesn't sound ungallant or ungrateful—we had sex at her instigation in a car in the restaurant parking lot. Once I was back in Charlottesville, Adrienne sent me the soundtrack from *Black Orpheus,* a Brazilian film we had seen in Los Angeles. Along with the album came a card: "I am a Eurydice you'll always be able to awaken."

It hadn't dawned on me until then that I had never been the only unregenerate romantic in the relationship. I didn't acknowledge the gift and happily went the next three decades without Adrienne Daly.

book three

CHAPTER FOURTEEN

Like any writer, I have faith in the efficacy of language, the power of words to move readers and shape reality. Although not entirely aware of it then, I realize now that I told Amy the story of my affair with her mother not simply to persuade her that I wasn't her father. I hoped to accomplish much more. In addition to showing her something about myself—okay, quite a lot about myself—I meant to give her a sense of her mother's character and of her own personal identity as well as a glimpse of the world she was born into. Perhaps I imagined that when I stopped speaking, she wouldn't need to know more; she'd feel that she was in full possession of the past.

But I failed and could do no better than console myself with a line from Flaubert's *Madame Bovary:* "Human speech is a cracked kettle on which we tap out crude rhythms for bears to dance to while we long to make music that will melt the stars." My narrative not only failed to melt the stars, it didn't even succeed in establishing the facts to Amy's satisfaction. Although too polite to accuse me of lying, she remained unconvinced by my denial of paternity, and she longed to know more about her mother.

"Are you in touch with her?" she asked.

"No. I haven't spoken to her in years."

"Do you have friends in common?"

"Acquaintances. I'm out of touch with them too."

"Than how can you be positive she's alive?"

"Your mother was interviewed on CNN a couple of weeks ago," I said. "I was channel surfing when I caught sight of her. Long as it's been, I recognized her right away."

"Why was she on CNN?" Amy asked and made a joke of it. "Is she a bareback rider in the circus, like I fantasized?"

I explained that Adrienne Daly (I told Amy her real name) had married into a wealthy, prominent family whose name was international in scope and constituted a well-known marketing label. She had gone on to a successful career in business and politics. Serving in various capacities as a presidential appointee, she had been an assistant secretary of state and later became an ambassador. In articles and interviews, she was still referred to as a diplomat and accorded the title of ambassador, and she skated back and forth between the private sector and presidential commissions, think tanks and policy committees.

Amy was stunned. Adrienne's life seemed flabbergasting to her, not just because she had money and social standing but because of her public persona. Celebrity, publicity, media attention were the last things Amy would have wanted for herself. She valued privacy and family and had told her fiancé, who entertained ambitions of running for political office, that she wanted no part of that. Still, she did want to meet her birth mother.

"Do you know how to reach Adrienne?" she asked, referring to her, as she always would, by her first name.

"I don't have an address or phone number, if that's what you mean. But I think I can find her."

"I'd appreciate that," she said.

In turn, I said I'd appreciate a favor from her. I made her promise to let me speak to Adrienne before she did. I regarded this as a favor to Amy more than to me. I feared how Adrienne might react if she heard from her daughter with no advance warning. There was every chance she'd say or do something hurtful.

Yet, as I set out to locate Adrienne by renewing old acquaintances, it was soon evident that I had opened myself up to hurt and embarrassment. People who recalled that things had ended badly between us were wary when I asked for her whereabouts. Others were amused by my interest in contacting a former girlfriend. Since I was calling from London, they wisecracked that I must be pretty hot to trot. Weren't things going well in my marriage? Was this a case of middle-aged craziness? Or some antic quest that I intended to turn into an article?

Since I couldn't tell them the truth, I invented lame excuses, none of which worked. Maybe Adrienne had fallen out of touch with them too. Maybe they just didn't care to get involved. No one admitted knowing where she was. Still, I kept calling around, and at the same time, I started a second search, this one for straight answers from the Children's Home Society.

CHS's postadoption program has a toll-free line whose answering machine invites callers to leave a name, message and telephone number. If it's "an emergency situation, please indicate such in your message." "Please note," the automated voice concludes, "CHS no longer provides adoption placement services."

When several days passed without a return call from CHS, I redialed the toll-free line and left word that mine was an emergency situation. I said I was a journalist on deadline doing a story about adoptions and needed to fact-check some material about the Children's Home Society.

This call too prompted no response, so I phoned CHS's executive offices in downtown Los Angeles and asked to speak to somebody in communications or public relations. Connected with Betty Moroz, I explained that I had dealt with CHS in 1964 when I had helped a young woman place her baby for adoption. Now I was planning to write about my experience—this possibility had, in fact, occurred to me—and I needed a history of the agency, verification of its procedures decades ago and an explanation of its current mission.

Ms. Moroz put me through to Amelia Nuñez-Wells, a woman of disarming warmth and patience who is the CEO of the Children's Home Society. I assured her that I wasn't trying to gain access that violated the agency's policies and had no desire to cause her or anyone else at CHS inconvenience. In addition to obtaining general background information, I just wanted to clarify several issues related to my personal experience.

Ms. Nuñez-Wells sounded more than receptive. Because of my previous dealings with CHS, she considered me a client, and as such, she said, I had a claim on the agency's resources. Indeed, since it no longer placed children for adoption, its lone mission was to provide services to adoptees, birth parents, adoptive parents and people like me who had been involved "in the process." "If there's anything we can do for you," she said, "just let me know."

When I said I didn't want to presume upon her generosity and valuable time and that I'd be glad to submit my questions to one of her employees, she swore it was no trouble. If I told her what I needed and gave her a week, she'd get me answers or steer me to the appropriate source.

I asked for the number of adoptions handled by CHS in 1964 and the number of reunions that it had been instrumental in arranging since then. Ms. Nuñez-Wells immediately emphasized that although the agency released "nonidentifying information," it wasn't for the purpose of arranging reunions. Under California law, former clients had the right to limited data from their files. She believed many adoptees were less interested in reuniting with birth parents than in learning about their ethnic origins and medical histories. Clients could submit Consent to Contact forms, but CHS didn't keep statistics on how often this resulted in a reunion.

I was curious about how the "nonidentifying information" was compiled. What was it based on? What controls existed to prevent the disclosure of inaccurate information and the identity of peripheral people? Did CHS have a file on me? If so, I said, I'd like to see it.

I also wanted to know how my name had wound up on Amy's birth certificate. Since the agency had urged me to sign an affidavit swearing I wasn't the father, how had this happened? Would it be willing to inform Amy that I wasn't her father?

Then it came to me that Adrienne's caseworker, the woman I called Mrs. Christian, might still be on the CHS staff. Even if she had retired, the agency could contact her and have her assure Amy that I was telling the truth.

"It's been so long," Ms. Nuñez-Wells said, "she's probably dead by now. Everything's changed since your day. Procedures, adoption practices and the law. Even the old building you describe, the white wooden one with the columns, doesn't exist anymore." Still, she promised that she'd look into everything and get back to me.

A week later, a CHS secretary phoned me to set up a conference call with Ms. Nuñez-Wells and one of her colleagues, someone specially qualified to address the questions I had raised. It seemed that I would soon have answers. It seemed that way right up until Donna Earll, the director of Community Education Services at CHS introduced herself.

Considerably less open to discussion and 20 degrees cooler than Ms. Nuñez-Wells, Ms. Earll told me that I had gone about my search all wrong. CHS rules called for inquiries to be submitted in writing. "As a former client requesting information, you're expected to abide by CHS policy," Ms. Earll said.

"What if I weren't a client? What if I were a journalist calling with questions."

"But you *are* a client."

"That's not something I was aware of until Ms. Nuñez-Wells told me. I don't expect preferential treatment, but I thought that clients would get better access."

Ms. Earll said she didn't have time to discuss the intricacies of adoption law over the phone. She suggested that I consult the *Manual of Policies and Procedures: The Adoption User's Manual,* which I could obtain from the California Department of Social Services warehouse. Meanwhile, to obtain the answers I needed from CHS, I would have to submit an itemized written request that should include the birth mother's name, the birth father's name if known, Amy's birth date and place of birth, and my notarized signature. If I cared to speed up the process, I could send all this by fax. But I shouldn't expect an answer in less than two weeks.

"What about general information? The number of adoptions and so forth? Can't you let me have that now?"

"No, not until we receive a written request."

Ms. Earll replied in a timely fashion, but not in a very helpful one. By mail she dispatched a copy of the affidavit I had signed at the CHS's urging. All "identifying information," as Ms. Earll referred to it, had been "redacted," so that the document in its entirety now read, "I,

Michael F. Mewshaw, am not the father of the baby born to _____ on
_____." The deleted name and date were the ones I had provided Ms.
Earll. Such a bowdlerized document wasn't likely to convince Amy of
anything.

Ms. Earll ended her letter, "Be assured that we are in the process of
researching answers to your additional questions and will be in contact
as soon as possible."

Days later, Ms. Nuñez-Wells wrote to say much the same thing. "Be
assured that we have reviewed your correspondence and will answer
your questions to the best of our ability." She urged me to call "to
arrange a time to personally talk to you."

It dawned on me that any frustration and inconvenience I might en-
counter couldn't compare to what adoptees must suffer as they cope
with the tangles of red tape that lie coiled between them and their birth
parents. Of course, it's a litigious society, and bureaucracies have to protect themselves. But some of the catch-22's in postadoption policy rival
the theater of the absurd.

When Ms. Nuñez-Wells, Ms. Earll and I had our next conference
call, they appeared to be playing good cop, bad cop. While Ms. Earll
snapped, "I don't understand," or "What's your question?" in answer to
almost everything I said, Ms. Nuñez-Wells sighed and wished she could
be more helpful but contended that California law handcuffed her. "We
make a legal and moral commitment to maintain confidentiality," she
said. "We're very traditional. And California is very conservative in this
regard."

What this meant, I pointed out to the two women, was that they
couldn't acknowledge what I already knew and they justified this on the
grounds that they needed to preserve confidentiality that no longer existed. Who was the Children's Home Society protecting? Was it possible

that, as with butt-covering government bureaucracies that classify everything as top secret, CHS just wanted to protect itself ?

Ms. Nuñez-Wells and Ms. Earll repeated that their hands were tied
by law. They maintained that they couldn't release material from their
files that discussed me by name. They could let me have only documents
that I had signed, and there was just one of those—the redacted affidavit.

Ms. Earll asserted that this benefited me since "we wouldn't divulge
anything about you either."

To the contrary, I argued, CHS had divulged a great deal about me,
some of it erroneous and potentially harmful. It was largely what Amy
had learned from the supposedly "nonidentifying information" that had
led her to me and, moreover, led her to believe that I was her father. Although I had been fortunate that this mistake had not adversely affected
my marriage and my family, I could imagine instances where it might,
and although Amy didn't have grasping motives, other searchers might
make trouble on the basis of botched information.

Ms. Earll claimed, as had Ms. Nuñez-Wells in our first conversation,
that "nonidentifying information" was not provided to adoptees to reunite them with their birth parents. It was just background.

"But that's what it's used for," I said. "And Amy's file was full of stuff
that went way beyond background."

"A lot of times a client gives a caseworker misleading information,"
Ms. Earll said. "We can't investigate everything a client tells us. So we include it in a general summary. That indicates to me the caseworker was
being diligent."

"Are you saying that's why CHS described a boyfriend who lived
with Adrienne—just to give Amy a full picture?"

"Yes," Ms. Nuñez-Wells chimed in. "We like to pass along as much
to an adoptee as we legally can. It can be a comfort to know what was

happening around the time of her birth, and especially to know that her mother wasn't alone."

If the goal was to comfort Amy, I asked, why did CHS mention the third man who had proposed to Adrienne? What was the relevance? Wouldn't that be more apt to confuse and upset her?

"What goes into the nonidentifying information," Ms. Earll said, "is what a birth mother shares with a caseworker. If there was a mention of three men who proposed marriage, then that's what's included."

Since it was obvious that not everything Adrienne had "shared" during a dozen counseling sessions had made it into a two-page summary, Ms. Nuñez-Wells conceded that thoroughness alone couldn't account for the mention of three men. It might have been intended to suggest, she admitted, some uncertainty about the true identity of Amy's biological father.

"But I don't want to speak specifically about this," Ms. Nuñez-Wells added, "because of confidentiality. Also, it was a long time ago, before either of us came to work at CHS. We now have different procedures for phrasing the nonidentifying information."

"How did it used to be done?" I asked. "Did a caseworker go back over her notes and write up a synopsis?"

"Sometimes it was the caseworker. Sometimes the caseworker had retired or died, and another person compiled the data."

It struck me that what would have been crucial to the original caseworker might, years later, not seem important to another person. It also occurred to me again that Adrienne's caseworker could clear up my questions. But when I asked about Mrs. Christian, I was informed that everything about her fell under the confidentiality rule. Whether she was alive or dead, whether she or someone else had assembled Amy's "nonidentifying information," was off limits.

I tried to reason with the women. I came close to begging. "I'm in a fix," I said. "Amy believes I'm her father because of mistakes made by the Children's Home Society. Why not correct those mistakes?"

Ms. Earll in her adamant fashion, Ms. Nuñez-Wells in her more amenable manner, both disagreed that CHS had made any mistakes. It had abided by its procedures and state law.

"That's not entirely true," I protested. "It can't be according to procedure and law to put the wrong name on a birth certificate."

Ms. Earll repeated that CHS depended on information supplied by the birth mother.

"But CHS knew the birth mother had provided inaccurate information. They had a signed affidavit swearing I wasn't the father."

Ms. Nuñez-Wells couldn't account for this. She acknowledged that it wasn't standard—in her words, it was "very unusual"—to demand an affidavit. She had no idea why I had been asked to sign one but concluded, "I don't think there are going to be answers to everything you ask because this all took place so long ago."

"Look, I'm not blaming anybody or considering legal action. I just want to understand how things went wrong, then figure out how to set them right."

This was difficult to do, however, since the two women refused to concede that the slightest thing was amiss. They insisted that CHS had gone by the book and had never broken its guarantee of confidentiality.

I suggested that they reread the "nonidentifying information." "All of it derived from Adrienne's counseling sessions," I said. "That seems to me to violate her privacy—unless you're claiming that adoption law supersedes a patient-therapist relationship and its privilege?"

"I think our clients understand that certain nonidentifying information will be released to adoptees," Ms. Nuñez-Wells said.

"But the information that CHS gave Amy *was* identifying. I'm not saying it was intentional, but when CHS revealed that her birth mother had been a runner-up in the Miss Maryland contest, it narrowed the field to a single state and reduced the pool of women from millions to a handful."

But neither Ms. Earll nor Ms. Nuñez-Wells would budge. The most Ms. Nuñez-Wells would allow was that there were now technical innovations—the Internet and so forth—that nobody could have anticipated.

"Amy didn't trace me over the Internet," I said. "She used your records and a Maryland phone directory."

That changed nothing in their opinion. My long conversation with the Children's Home Society ended with me learning a huge amount about its monolithic mind-set, but nothing at all that would help me with Amy.

CHAPTER FIFTEEN

In fiction and on film, journalists have acquired a swashbuckling image. In hot pursuit of the truth, they appear to run a constant gauntlet of car chases, sexual temptations and hair-raising close calls. But the mundane fact is that most investigative reporting these days takes place at a computer terminal. The excitement of the hunt and the satisfaction of a scoop are more like the experiences of a research librarian than a classic hard-boiled private eye.

But shameful as it is to admit, even a librarian's triumphs were denied me. Computer-illiterate and despairing of finding her through friends, I had to have a helper search for Adrienne Daly via the Internet. In a matter of days, I received a batch of newspaper and magazine clippings, many with datelines in Kuala Lumpur, Beijing, Seoul, Tokyo and Singapore. Whether traveling for business or as a U.S. government representative, Adrienne spoke authoritatively on a broad spectrum of subjects ranging from telecommunications to terrorism, from Islamic splinter sects to the feasibility of an intellectual Marshall Plan in Eastern Europe. Depicted by the press as a contemporary woman-on-the-go, she was said to have seamlessly combined the roles of wife, mother, homemaker, entrepreneur and public servant.

The photos accompanying the articles presented a well-groomed, well-coiffed woman—her hair was still dark but now cut short—who had kept her figure and her looks. No longer a beauty queen or an in-genue, she projected the quiet strength of a high achiever, well aware of her talent and convinced that others should recognize it too. A profile in the *New York Times* characterized her as "a tough cookie" whose col-leagues referred to her behind her back as "the Iron Magnolia." Full of "confidence and managerial skill," she was said to be "interested in ad-vancing her own cause . . . and effective in doing that." In response to criticism, Adrienne told a reporter, "If being liked is your ultimate goal, you don't belong in the public policy forum."

If nothing else, this suggested that she had changed enormously since our days together, when she had implored me to arrange the adoption, fretted about everybody's opinion and craved validation from the most improbable people. Before each appointment with her obstetrician in LA, she used to insist on forty-eight hours of abstinence because she didn't want the doctor to know that she was sexually active.

Along with updates of her résumé and her *Who's Who* entry, Lexis-Nexis contained half-a-dozen real estate transactions involving Adri-enne and her husband. They owned homes in the Washington suburbs, in the Rocky Mountains, on the coast of California and at a ski resort. In addition to the cost of each house and the address, there was a list of telephone numbers. All I had to do was dial.

At every number, in three different time zones, an answering service instructed me to leave a message. The voice was a man's—Adrienne's husband or son, I presumed. That made me reluctant to leave my name and number. I didn't care to hear from the wrong member of the Daly clan, and since I was in London, there was the time difference to consider. I didn't want to get a call in the middle of the night or again in the middle of a family dinner.

After such a long silence, after so many surprises in the past, I couldn't hazard a guess what Adrienne might do or say once I had her on the line. But I kept dialing. This went on for weeks. Starting in the late afternoon, I would station myself at the kitchen table, which had a west-facing window. With Marc at school and Linda hours away from fixing dinner, I had the room to myself. On clear days, the sunsets were astonishing, the sky ribbed with pink and orange bands. Nothing I saw from where I sat reminded me of my childhood. Neither the sunsets in California nor those in Maryland had looked like this, and it struck me, not for the first time, that that was why I lived outside the United States. There was a lot that I didn't care to be reminded of.

Finally someone picked up in Bethesda. Even as a college coed, Adrienne had had a distinctly crisp telephone voice. I used to razz her that she sounded like a receptionist for U.S. Steel. But when I said, "This is Mike Mewshaw," the corporate ice melted.

"I can't believe it. How long's it been?"

"A long, long time."

"To what do I owe this honor?" she asked, then, without waiting for an answer, she said, "You're lucky to catch me here. I'm usually out West. I've been on the road for weeks. I just got back from China. I'm not sure I'm coherent. I have a bad cold and a terminal case of jet lag."

She didn't sound sick or exhausted, just slightly giddy and bemused. She asked where I was calling from. Why was I in London? How long had I lived there? She had read an interview with me from Rome and assumed I was still based in Italy. We traded pleasantries for a few minutes before she got around to asking again why I had called.

"The baby we left in Los Angeles," I said. "Her name is Amy. She's been in touch with me and believes I'm her father."

Adrienne made a sound. A sigh or a groan.

"It's worse than that," I said. "She called my sister first and thought Karen was her mother."

"What did you tell her?"

"The truth. But I can't seem to convince her."

"Of what?"

"That I'm not her father. I told her about us, our time in California. But she doesn't believe me."

"Did you tell her about me?"

"Yes, but I said not to contact you until we had had a chance to talk."

"Why'd you do that?"

Assuming she was upset that I had put Amy off, I explained that I'd done it to give Adrienne a chance to absorb the news and to choose a convenient time for them to speak.

"But why did you tell her my name?" she demanded. "How could you do that to me, Mike? Don't I deserve the simple courtesy of deciding for myself whether I welcome contact with her?"

"Under the circumstances—" I fought to keep my voice neutral—"I didn't think you'd mind talking to her."

"I thought I could count on you. No matter how things ended between us, I thought you'd understand what it's like to spend half a lifetime trying to forget this."

"Do you feel it's fair that my family and I have to deal with it and you don't?"

"You're jumping to the conclusion that anybody has to deal with it. You could have told this woman she had the wrong number. You're not her father. Period!"

"You don't think she deserves better than that?"

"I don't know what she deserves, Mike. I don't know, and neither do you, whether she is who she claims to be."

Trying to calm Adrienne, and struggling to stay cool myself—she spoke to me like an underling, some summer intern who had muffed an assignment—I admitted that I too had been suspicious of Amy and had confided nothing until after I had verified her story. Everything had checked out, including the "nonidentifying information," which was accurate in every respect.

"She could have gotten that file by fraud or bribery," Adrienne protested.

"I spoke to the woman who brought her up. She described the adoption and how Amy went about searching for her biological parents."

"That doesn't prove anything. The two of them could be in this together, pulling some sort of scam. Out to make trouble or, more likely, make money."

"That's not my impression," I said. "They sound very likeable and trustworthy. But don't take my word for it. Call her and make up your own mind. If she starts making threats or demands, all you have to do is hang up."

"Oh, Mike." She sounded close to tears. For an instant, I feared she'd hang up on me. Instead, she asked whether Amy was married. Did she have children? Was she educated? What was her profession?

I repeated what Amy and Mrs. Woodson had told me. I stressed, as Amy had, that she didn't expect a public acknowledgement or contact with Adrienne's family. "She has her own family and says she had a happy childhood."

"Then why's she so anxious to track down her biological parents? I don't have to remind you that there are crazy kids in this world. Think of your friend, the guy who killed his adoptive parents."

"Are you really afraid your daughter's out to get you?"

"Like anyone in the public eye and with a bit of money, I've had crank calls and letters."

"Look, trust me, whoever Amy is, I don't see her as a killer."

"You've seen her?"

"A photograph. She looks like you."

"I don't look the way you remember me. I've had two kids. I've been married to the same man for almost thirty years. I'm a middle-aged matron."

"Does your husband know about Amy?" It didn't occur to me to ask whether he knew about me.

"Yes, of course," she said. "I told him before we married. But my children don't know, and I don't think they could handle it."

"My sons have. I told them, and there's been no problem. Look, I realize this is hard—"

"You don't have any idea how hard." She explained that her son, now in his midtwenties, was angry and rebellious, and this was the sort of news that might rile him up. As for her daughter, she was in delicate health. She had a serious degenerative condition and was slowly going blind.

Alarmed, I told Adrienne of Amy's primary concern. Before she had children, she needed to know the family medical history. If nothing else, Adrienne owed her that much.

"I already have my hands full," she said. "I can't cope with more doctor talk and discussions of hereditary illnesses and handicaps." Then she broke it to me that she suffered from lupus. Although it was in remission at present, she hoped I understood why a reunion with Amy wasn't one of her priorities.

It saddened me to hear of Adrienne's ill health, and I realized that her daughter's condition caused her even more anguish. What parent doesn't agonize over every setback, every sickness, that children suffer? But along

with an effusion of compassion, there floated over me an unnerving feeling that I had been through this before with Adrienne, who had often
played on my sympathy. It was difficult to separate two images of her in my
mind—that of a conscientious mother, with her own compromised health,
grieving over her daughter's blindness, and that of the globe-trotting executive and diplomat who had just returned from China.

"I've seen you on TV," I said. "You look like you're holding up very
well to me."

She accepted this as flattery rather than a not-so-subtle reminder that
her medical condition didn't prevent her from meeting a full calendar of
business commitments. She said she was glad her aches and pains hadn't
made her unrecognizable to me.

"No, in that interview on CNN, you appeared to be in splendid
shape," I said.

"How could you tell? I was sitting down."

"I could see your legs."

"That's what Henry Kissinger always says about Margaret Thatcher—
great legs. You know, Mike, I think about you. When I'm traveling, I
keep expecting to bump into you at an airport in some godforsaken
place." She mentioned a few pieces I'd done for the *New York Times* on
cities she had visited. She called it an interesting coincidence that she
had honeymooned in Morocco, which was the setting of my third
novel. "Wouldn't it have been fun," she said, "if we had run into each
other at the Mamounia? Do you still write books? I haven't noticed any
reviews lately."

This hurt, as, I suppose, it was meant to. "Yeah, when the rent's due
and we get hungry, I crank one out."

"I stopped reading your novels a long time ago. They made me look
like such a B-I-T-C-H," she spelled it out. "Is that how you think of me?"

"That's one of the ways I think of you. But there are others."

"From what I've seen of your books, nobody would know that. Am I such a terrible person?"

"I didn't say that."

"Yes, you did. You wrote it in your novels."

"You just admitted you haven't read them for years."

"My husband warned me not to bother with your latest. He said it would just make me sad. And I don't need that. I've had enough sadness. I've had to live with my decision about the baby, and even though I believe I made the right choice, it's been painful."

"I'm sorry. I know it must have been. And if anything in my novels hurt you, I'm sorry about that too. But you've got to understand that they're fiction, not fact."

Adrienne replied that whether in fiction or fact, it seemed to her unfair to be forced to revisit the past. "I thought it was better to have the baby and give it up than to have an abortion or to marry Dave and make everybody miserable. Can you honestly claim that things haven't worked out the way they should have, the way that's best for everybody?"

"I can't speak for everybody."

"Then speak for yourself. You seem to have had a good life. You've become a writer, which is what you wanted. You tell me Amy had a happy childhood. Speaking for myself, I haven't done too badly. I was raised to believe in giving something back, and I've made my contribution." As if she doubted that I was aware of her achievements, she summarized her CV.

"That's mighty impressive," I deadpanned.

"Do I hear sarcasm? You've always had this knack for making me feel worthless."

"I disagree. My memory is of spending five or six months doing everything in my power to make you feel good about yourself. If I thought you were worthless, why would I have done that? Why would I have wanted to marry you?"

"That's the problem, isn't it? That's why I'm being punished. I wouldn't marry you. You'll never forgive me for that."

I protested that I had no intention of punishing her and bore her no ill will. "We both have our version of the past," I said, "and we're too old to argue over what happened way back when. You've been successful and have a right to be proud. If you're satisfied with your decisions, that's fine. But what I called you about is the here and now. Amy needs to know—"

"You caught me at a bad time," she broke in apologetically. "I'm tired. I don't feel well, and the cold medicine makes me . . . I don't know, not myself. On top of that, do you realize where I am now?"

"Maryland."

"I mean precisely where I am. I'm in my parents' house."

A picture loomed up of a tree-shaded lane, an incongruous Spanish Provincial in a neighborhood of Cape Cod and colonial homes, an interior full of oriental bric-a-brac, a foldout bed in her father's office where Adrienne and I had slept when the Dalys were away. "Are your parents there?" I asked.

"No. Daddy died in the '80s. Mother died a few years ago. I bought my brother's share of the house. When I was with the State Department, commuting from out West a couple of times a month became a hardship for the family. So for a few years we lived here. Afterward, I decided to keep the place. Guess where I'm sitting."

I couldn't.

"On the staircase that leads up to my old bedroom. Remember?" In no mood for a stroll down memory lane, I didn't reply. When Adrienne's voice softened and she started reminiscing, I suspected her of sidetracking us.

"I stood on these stairs," she said, "the day you took back all the love letters you wrote me. You ripped them to pieces right in front of me. You were so angry."

"I wonder why?" I asked.

"Remember that time in the car when you hit me?"

"I do, and it's not a pretty picture. I'd be glad to apologize and go over all this with you once we've discussed what to do about Amy."

"I bet you wish you had those letters now to see how well you wrote at that age. Even then you were very literary. I loved your letters."

"Look, Adrienne, I don't mean to be rude or to hurt you—"

"Oh, Mike, I always thought you hurt yourself more than you hurt me. When I flew to China, we took off from LAX and passed over Catalina. Remember Catalina? Remember Mexico?"

I won't maintain that these memories had no meaning for me. I had, after all, related many of them to Amy. But they also made me impatient, not just with Adrienne but with myself, the naïf I had been and the fool I was afraid of being now.

"I traveled to Mexico a few years ago with a delegation from Asia," she said. "One night over drinks I told them I had been there before when I was twenty-one and slept on the beach with a boy I loved. Weren't you scared? they wanted to know. I told them, no, I felt safe with him."

"Adrienne," I interrupted, "are you going to talk to Amy or aren't you?"

"I don't know. I can't promise anything. But let me have her phone number and I'll think it over."

"Do me a favor," I said. "Tell her the truth. Tell her I'm not her father."

Outside the kitchen window, the sky, except for a red line at the horizon, had gone dark. White birds flickered through my field of vision like Paracletes bearing some inscrutable message. But they were seagulls, miles from the ocean, scavenging for a meal in the suburbs. It was garbage night in Hampstead.

CHAPTER SIXTEEN

For more than a year, Amy and I continued to exchange cards and phone calls. No matter what else we discussed, the subject always circled around to Adrienne. Had she contacted Amy? No, she still hadn't. Had I spoken to her again? No, not so far.

Although disappointed not to have heard from her birth mother, Amy didn't sound angry. Her voice, which apart from her snapshot was all I knew of her, remained resolutely upbeat. "I'm a happy person," she repeated. "I have a happy life. It's just that I'm having a few physical problems, and it might help the doctors if I could give them more background."

Until then, it had seemed sensible not to pass along hearsay about Adrienne's lupus and her daughter's blindness. If it was untrue or exaggerated, I didn't want to alarm Amy. Better for her to receive an accurate account from Adrienne than a garbled one from me. But now that she mentioned medical problems, I felt duty-bound to fill her in on what Adrienne had said.

I also gave her the name of her biological father, figuring that she deserved to have Dave's medical history as well. Again, I was going on Adrienne's word, which hadn't always proved reliable. Since the Children's Home Society had seen fit to mention a third man, I supposed there was room for doubt.

When Amy asked whether I knew how to reach Dave, I said that I didn't. Nor did I volunteer to find him. At least with Adrienne I shared a personal vocabulary and a past that made conversation possible. With Dave, I had just one thing in common: we had both loved the same woman. Actually, there was a second thing: we had both been dumped by her. But I suspected that he blamed me for that, and I didn't relish the idea of another telephone conversation that rehashed the trouble I had caused.

Still, I felt I should have done something more for Amy. After all, I knew what it was like to believe that an answer lay tantalizingly beyond your fingertips, to fear that central people in your life would remain forever out of touch. I knew what it was to search in vain, to wait with little hope and to lose what you thought you loved. But besides talk, what could I offer Amy?

For several months, silence seemed the best course, detachment the correct decision. Then in May, Amy announced that she and Jason (as I'll call him), her fiancé, were getting married and flying to Europe for a honeymoon that would take them from Paris to the south of France and Italy. For a few minutes, we discussed meeting somewhere on their itinerary. In the end, though, we agreed that they shouldn't waste a moment of their wedding trip on a stranger who, through bizarre happenstance, had once known her birth mother.

"Can I ask you something?" she said. "Please, tell me the truth. Are you my father?"

I swore that I wasn't.

"It'd be so great if you were. At least you'll talk to me." Adrienne still hadn't called her, and Amy hadn't been able to locate her biological father.

Wanting to end on a happy note, I congratulated her on the wedding and wished her the best of luck.

"We do have to meet someday," she said. "Jason wonders who this man in my life is."

"I'm sure our paths will cross," I said, not at all positive that it would ever happen.

But much sooner than expected, an opportunity presented itself. My older son, Sean, moved to Los Angeles. Late that summer, eager to visit him, I caught a nonstop flight from London that passed over the North Pole and allowed fourteen hours of droning white noise in which to meditate on the meaning of California in my family history.

At the age of three, I had made my first trek west with my five-year-old brother, my mother, then pregnant with Karen, and the man I referred to as Tommy or Dad, according to the occasion. Aboard a Greyhound bus crammed with servicemen who had mustered out of uniform after World War II, the trip took the better part of a week. Or I should say the worst part of a week.

Everything about that marathon bus ride was off-kilter and out of synch. Tommy smelled of what I didn't know was whiskey, and he dozed for hours, hungover and drooling. Mom and he argued in vicious whispers, and I couldn't sleep at night. Then during the day, I couldn't stay awake. When we stopped for meals at some greasy spoon, I had no appetite. Later, as we crossed endless stretches of scrubby desert, I sobbed with hunger pangs and complained that I had to pee. Remarkably, Mom never lost her temper. Cuddling me on her lap, she soothed me with what sounded like fairy tales. We were headed for a paradise where the sun always shone, she said. Where the mountains were snow-capped year-round, orange groves grew in the valleys and palm trees waved in ocean breezes.

What I wouldn't learn until after Tommy was dead and Mom was in her eighties was that the two of them weren't married. There's no evidence that they ever exchanged vows in a church or courthouse. It's likely that all the years Tommy lived with us, he was still married to a woman in Ohio by whom he had other children. When I learned this in my late fifties, it dawned on me why Mom had always been so secretive, sick with worry and sadness. Convinced that she was living in sin, she had urged me to stand by Adrienne while the baby was born because our predicament recalled her own—pregnant, unwed, drifting west.

My family's life in California lasted a short, disastrous period. Tommy interviewed for a job selling Schick razor blades but was told that he had the wrong clothes, and unless he got his teeth fixed, he wasn't fit to do anything except manual labor. Drunk, he threatened to abandon us and hitchhike back East. It might have been better for everybody if he had. Instead, unable to afford bus tickets for the return trip, the four of us joined a man who was headed for Washington, D.C., in a rusty Packard and welcomed paying passengers.

That early misconceived move to Los Angeles should have served as aversion therapy. Yet for me, California remained talismanic. It was the place I traveled to over and over, fervently trusting it would solve my problems. I had been there a dozen times before I had joined Adrienne in LA. Like a bird hardwired to migrate in a set pattern, I imitated my family's original trek west, then the defeated retreat east. Now that my son had settled in the golden land of second chances, new starts and reinvented lives, I hoped that it would work out for him.

During the long flight, it hit me how easily everything might have been different. If my family had stayed in LA in the 1940s, I would never have met Adrienne, and Amy wouldn't be living in California today. Maybe she wouldn't have been born at all. Or if Adrienne had moved north or south and put the baby up for adoption in Boston or Miami, Amy would have led an utterly different life. But about one thing I no longer harbored any illusions. After talking with Adrienne, I didn't believe it would have worked out between us no matter where we lived.

When the plane landed that afternoon at LAX, it was freakishly hot, more like the Sahara than Southern California. On the road in from the airport, the palm fronds were brown. Tossed by a desert wind, they resembled unimaginably tall dandelions that had gone to seed.

Having departed London in a cool morning drizzle, I was staggered by jet lag as well as the heat. Checking into a hotel near Sunset Boulevard, several blocks from where Adrienne and I had lived, I planned to get some sleep, but I made the mistake of placing a call to Amy before I lay down.

She had spoken to her birth mother. The news sizzled through me like meth. Suddenly wide awake, I had to hear the details. But Amy was late for an appointment. We agreed to meet for lunch the next day and talk once I had acclimated.

The process of acclimation, I discovered, wouldn't permit sleep. So I showered, changed clothes and went for a walk, trying to tire myself to the point of exhaustion I had felt twenty minutes ago. Yet whatever else it may have to recommend it, a stroll along Sunset Strip isn't soporific. With the sun like molten lava on my back, I let it all flow over me—the glitz and kitsch, the hamburger joints and four-star restaurants, the boutique windows full of erotic toys, Rolls-Royces and Scientology brochures. The Body Shop was still in business, as was the Chateau Marmont, its shabby gentility of my day having given way to swank gentrification.

Ambling downhill on North Harper Street, I felt that my endless afternoon in the air and the torrid wind had conspired to fry my synapses. Baudelaire once wrote, "No human heart changes half so fast as the face of a city." But this part of Los Angeles didn't appear to have changed at all. Standing in front of our former address, I was struck by how much the apartment building with its stucco facade, red tiles and wrought-iron grillwork resembled the Daly house back in Bethesda, where Adrienne still lived part-time.

Continuing down North Harper and swinging west on Delongpre, past Loretta Young's old house, I thought the neighborhood should have felt haunted. But it didn't stoke up any of the nostalgia that sometimes seized me in London or Rome or Madrid. The boy I had been here had become a foreigner. Maybe that was something I should tell Amy when we met. When you set out on a quest, there isn't just the risk that you'll fail. There's the risk that you'll retrace your steps to the place where you once lived and realize you never belonged there.

M y son had booked me into a hotel favored by film people and wannabes in that world. Since his girlfriend worked in the industry, I received a discount, a corner suite and a basket of fruit. But neither the bellhops—all apprentice actors—nor the receptionist—a Nicole Kidman look-alike—viewed me as a potential star maker. Although I had stayed in this same hotel over the years on screenwriting assignments, I was manifestly too square to merit a second glance.

When Amy arrived for lunch, though, everything changed. The parking valet eyed her as if she had to be that starlet whose name he knew but couldn't call to mind. Her progress through the lobby caused a palpable stir. More than merely beautiful, she had a kind of elegant carriage and physical presence that neither her snapshot nor her sweet phone voice had led me to expect.

She had on a black linen dress and sandals. Pushing a pair of sunglasses up to the crown of her head, she smiled and offered me her hand to shake. It was tempting to blurt, You look just like your mother. But that wasn't quite true. She was more like the platonic conception of Adrienne, the updated, streamlined version. Bare-armed and bare-legged, she had a creamy brown complexion. While her hair was as dark and straight as Adrienne's had been, Amy wore hers down to her shoulders, framing her face, which with its strong jaw and high cheekbones was somehow leaner than her mother's, yet softer at the same time. I didn't remember Dave well enough to judge what she had inherited from her father. Maybe his down-to-earth personality. Still, I recognized her mouth, the shape of her lips, their mobility as she spoke, the way they drew back at one corner as though she were about to confide a secret or crack a joke. That was Adrienne.

We lunched outside by the pool, shaded by a white canvas umbrella that smelled like a sail baked by the sun. Amy ordered a Cobb salad and iced tea. With my body clock in a state of breakdown—for me it was 10 P.M. Greenwich mean time—I had what amounted to an after-dinner cup of coffee. Talkative by nature, I'm afraid that the caffeine made me even more loquacious, but I can't recall a single word I said. I must have told her that Adrienne and I had lived nearby. When she mentioned that she and her husband owned a home in Pasadena, I must have told her that that had been part of my territory when I had sold business machines for Friden Inc. I must have told her that Sean lived in LA and it looked likely I'd come here often.

But I wouldn't swear to any of this. All I remember with clarity was what Amy said and how I felt. The two weren't necessarily connected.

Or maybe they were linked in the same dissonant fashion as Amy's fierce beauty and her vulnerability.

She told me that after I had given her Adrienne's name, she had gone to the local library on the pretense of doing research for a school project. That was how, she reminded me, a friend of hers had persuaded California Lutheran Hospital to provide the name from Amy's original birth certificate—by claiming to be a grad student. When Amy explained that she was writing a paper on Adrienne Daly, the librarian had supplied a batch of material from microfiche. Some of this surely replicated the newspaper and magazine articles that had been downloaded for me on Lexis-Nexis.

"Soon as I saw Adrienne's picture," Amy said, "there was no question." She set down her fork and spread her fingers. "Even our hands are the same. That was the strangest feeling—to see her hand and realize that for the first time in my life, I was looking at somebody related to me, someone just like me. I won't feel that again until I have my own kids."

Although her birth mother's photograph had lifted Amy's spirits, it had also left her impatient with the wait for Adrienne's call. She seemed so close that Amy felt frustrated in a passive role.

"I figured she might be tormented or at least curious about what happened after she gave me up," Amy said. "And I could assure her everything's okay. I've had a good life, and I don't hold anything against her. As a matter of fact, I'd like to thank her for letting me be born. I realize abortion was illegal back then, but she could have found somebody to do it. Or she could have thrown herself down a flight of stairs. Women do that," she said. "So I'm grateful to her."

Not far from us in the pool, a couple of men and a girl in a bikini swam desultory laps. The glare from the water forced me to move my chair. The hypnotic back-and-forth motion of the swimmers reminded me of the men mowing the grass outside Mrs. Christian's window the day she had cautioned me not to count on marrying Adrienne. Like so many momentous incidents in my life, this one seemed an odd tableau. A hotel in Hollywood, in 100-degree heat. An almost untouched Cobb salad on the table. A lovely woman spilling her guts to a white-haired gent who was jangled by coffee.

Amy said she had started calling Adrienne's numbers. As had been the case with me, no one was at home. The answering service instructed her to leave a message, but she couldn't bring herself to do that. After a few weeks, somebody picked up and informed her that Adrienne was in California. So Amy phoned there and finally got through.

"I introduced myself like they teach you to do at ALMA," she said. "I suggested that she write down my name and number in case we got cut off. They tell you to do that in case your birth parent hangs up in shock but reconsiders and decides to call back. Then I asked, 'Did you give a baby up for adoption in 1964?'"

"Adrienne said, 'I'm on the other line. I'll call you back.' It took her ten minutes. It felt to me like ten hours. But she did call back, and I told her I had reason to believe she was my biological mother."

Amy shoved aside her salad plate. "She said, 'This isn't a good time for me to talk.' Not then, not where she was. But she was going to be in California again later on, and she promised we could talk then. That was it. End of conversation."

"She didn't acknowledge she's your mother?"

"No."

"She didn't say I'm not your father?"

"I didn't have a chance to ask. I didn't even get to thank her for being born and to tell her I understand she did the hardest thing in the world for a woman to do. I'm not sure she'd care if I said it. She sounded so businesslike."

"That's just her phone manner. She's a better person than that.You'll agree once you meet her."

"*If* I meet her. I can't say whether I want to—not after the way she acted.When I started this search, I made up my mind I'd never force myself on my birth parents. I realized there was a chance I wouldn't find them, or it wouldn't work out if I did. So it shocks me how rejected I feel—like having let me go once, she's doing it again. If I wasn't worried about my medical history and about bringing babies into the world without a chance for a full life, I'd give up now."

"I'm sure she'll get in touch with you," I said.

"I guess I can live with it if she doesn't.At least I have you."

She. Had. Me. In my ears the words sounded spaced for emphasis. Part of me wanted to reply that despite a wife and two sons, despite all that Amy might imagine, nobody had me. Since my escapade with her mother, I had worked overtime to make myself a free agent.A man with no strings attached and bulletproofed against disappointment. But the truth was that ever since I had first spoken to Amy, I'd had a feeling that eluded definition. I used to boast that like most men, I can express any emotion—as long as it's anger. Now my every emotion seemed transmuted into melancholy and wistful yearning.

Yearning for what? I wondered. For the man I used to be? For a woman like the one in front of me? For a chance to undo or redo the past?

As if reading my thoughts,Amy asked, "Do you still love Adrienne?"

This had the ring of a test question, the sort a wily child might ask a parent about his spouse. Evasion seemed advisable. "I haven't seen her in a long time."

"You don't need to see somebody to love them." She mentioned kids she'd been out of touch with but whom she continued to love.

"No, I don't love her," I said. "If I have any feeling left, it's for the person she was, for the kids we were. And for what might have been."

"I'm sorry," Amy said.

"No need to be sorry. I'd feel differently about Adrienne if she'd been welcoming to you." I might have added, but didn't, that I was ashamed of Adrienne and ashamed of myself for having loved a woman who would treat Amy this way.

When lunch was over and we were waiting for the parking valet, Amy said, "Can I have a hug?"

I gladly gave her one and was sad to let her go.

CHAPTER SEVENTEEN

As I've written, my courtship of Adrienne Daly had consisted at first primarily of words—long talks, letters, the books we read together. To paraphrase Shakespeare on Othello's courtship of Desdemona, I wooed her through the ear. It would have been wise of me to keep in mind that that romance ended with Othello smothering Desdemona in a fit of jealousy. But at the time, words seemed all I had to offer, my one hope of attracting a woman who had so many other men clamoring for her favor.

Older now, I'd like to believe I wouldn't make the same mistake. Yet in the months after I met Amy, I found myself falling into my former role with Adrienne. By telephone, I talked to her. I asked questions and listened. I told her what I was writing. We discussed Islam, aging and our families. After I traveled to Uzbekistan for the *New York Times,* we swapped anecdotes about Central Asia—Tashkent, Samarkand and Bukhara, places where Adrienne had also been.

To a fair-minded observer, we might have sounded like college class-mates catching up on news. Nothing deeper than that. Once she warmed to a subject, Adrienne was willing to stay on the line as long as I did. I can't guess what she got out of these transatlantic gabfests. I can only be sure of my own intentions. I was out to seduce Adrienne, woo-ing her through the ear again.

Not that I wanted her to love me. I had something more conniving in mind. I wanted to break through her guard, insinuate myself into her confidence and persuade her to do two things: speak to Amy and tell her the truth about me.

It's possible that she was playing a double game. She had to be aware of what I was after since I so often swerved back to the subject. But maybe she was ready to indulge me as long as she got a chance to score her points. Sometimes our conversations juddered along like colliding monologues. When I complained that it was cruel of her to keep Amy in the dark and to keep me in a false position—why not simply tell Amy I wasn't her father?—Adrienne repeated that her family and her pro-fessional responsibilities came first. She took pains—or was it pride?—to update me on her busy schedule. She described a panel she served on with Colin Powell and recounted a junket to Africa during which she had gone water-skiing on the Congo River, then caught a hop on a C-130 to terror-plagued Algeria. Wherever she traveled, she said, she had to contend with DCMs and station chiefs and intelligence agents who played rough and liked to roll people from the State Department. But she maintained that she couldn't be rolled—by which I inferred she was serving notice that she wouldn't be bulldozed by me.

Yet if Adrienne could be brisk and self-important, there were also moments when, unprompted by anything I said, she became sentimen-tal and tender. She regretted that her son had never had a love affair like ours. "Young people today don't seem to be as serious as we were at twenty-one," she said. "They're more casual about sex and love and marriage."

I spotted an opening. "What if your son was in the situation we were in? What would you advise?"

"What do you mean?" Adrienne asked. "Which situation?"

"Say he was a junior in college, and his girlfriend was pregnant by another guy. What would you advise that they do?"

"It would depend on whether he loved her, and on how much she loved him."

"Let's assume that he loved her a lot," I said. "And his girlfriend claimed she loved him. Would you recommend that he drop out of school and stay with her while the baby was born?"

Adrienne might have objected that no two relationships are alike, or that I was loading the question. But she didn't equivocate. "I'd tell him if he loved her, he should help her. What would you say to your son?"

"I'd tell him there's a better way to go about it. I'd encourage him to give his girlfriend six months to straighten out her life, then see where they were afterward."

"What if he didn't listen to you? You were pretty headstrong at that age, Mike. Would you have let anybody, especially your parents, tell you what to do?"

"I wish I had had parents whose judgment I trusted."

"You mean you wish somebody had told you not to stay with me?"

"What I wish is that I had had somebody to talk to. The same holds true for you. Don't you think it would have helped to have had someone to discuss things with?"

"I had you," she said. "You had me. That seemed enough."

This was something I might have said as a lovesick college boy. It sounded out of character for Adrienne, the hardheaded pragmatist.

"If my son wouldn't listen to me," I said, "I'd go to the girl. I'd explain that they ought to think it over. They weren't being objective."

Adrienne hooted. "Look who's talking about being objective!"

I chuckled too. "Okay, do what I say. Not what I do. Not what I did. But I'd point out that living together in those circumstances could make it less likely that things would work for them."

"And if she didn't listen to you either?"

"Then I'd talk to her parents and try to get the two families on the same page."

"Yes, and your son would hate you for the rest of his life. And he and his girl would go ahead anyway and do as they pleased. Look, Mike, we were twenty-one and in love. I'm not sorry for doing what we did. It just didn't work out."

"No, I guess it didn't," I said, although in my opinion, "just" didn't cover half of it. But I didn't own up to this. I was too busy with my wooing campaign.

After all the calls I made, I finally received one. On our answering service, a woman with a theatrical British accent declared, "The Catalina Island Society will be meeting this Saturday. Please call to confirm whether you can attend." She left a London phone number and an extension. No name. But I knew. The coy reference to Catalina gave her away.

When I reached her at her hotel, Adrienne started in as if our transatlantic talks had served their purpose and we could now resume in person. She had been on the road for five weeks, flying from the States to South America on business, then to Asia for a combination of business and pleasure. On the return trip, she had decided to touch down in London. The previous night, she had gone to a dinner party where

Prince Michael, "a charming man," had been seated beside her. The day after tomorrow, she had an appointment in Oxford. If I didn't mind being squeezed in, she'd like to have lunch with me tomorrow.

"You'll be seeing me at my worst," she said. "I'm exhausted, and if that's not bad enough, the airline lost my luggage. I had to buy a replacement wardrobe at Marks & Spencer."

I thought my campaign had worked. But when I asked whether she had been in touch with Amy, she told me we'd talk about that the next day.

"And Mike," she said, "please bring along those adoption files."

The moment I hung up, I had misgivings. I felt I had been too eager to please, too willing to go along with the pretense that there was no disagreement between us. I considered calling back and rescheduling our meeting as a business appointment, not a social get-together. After all, she owed me an explanation. Several of them.

Yet I knew I wouldn't miss this for the world. It was a climactic scene no novelist could duck. The final chapter. The last installment of a reality show in which a man encounters an ex-lover and tests old wounds to see which, if any, still bleed.

But when Linda confronted me, I maintained that I was doing it for Amy. To arrange a reunion with her birth mother. To convince Adrienne to identify the birth father.

"There's more to it than that," Linda argued.

"Well, I am eager to see how far off base I was in my estimate of what would become of Adrienne."

"What did you expect?"

"By this stage of her life, I thought she'd be one of those alcoholic women who's been married five times and has a slew of neglected, neurotic kids and a miserable husband."

"That sounds like a Technicolor revenge fantasy—how you wished she had ended up."

"No, not really. I dreaded that her life might turn into a disaster. That's why I stayed with her. Part of the reason. To make sure she didn't foul herself up for good."

"Aren't you noble," Linda taunted me.

"Okay, there was some self-interest. When she got pregnant, I wanted to give her a chance to prove it was me she loved all along."

"Fooled you, didn't she?"

"In a lot more ways than I probably know even now. But nothing fooled me more than what she's become. After California, I didn't believe she'd ever get herself together."

"Maybe she found another man to rescue her. What interests me is what she would have predicted for you."

"I don't think she knew me well enough to guess. That's another reason to meet her tomorrow—to introduce myself."

B ecause I was supposed to play tennis later in the day, I packed my racket and clothes in a carry bag that Linda wisecracked looked big enough to hold everything I'd need for a week. "Are you creating a sporty image to prove you still have what it takes?"

"Adrienne was never impressed by my athleticism. She saw me play basketball once and said I looked like a hoodlum."

"Well, tennis is a more upscale game. Maybe she'll think you've put your juvenile-delinquent days behind you."

"This gives me an excuse to cut things short. If it gets uncomfortable, I'll tell her it's time for my match."

With a tennis racket as one prop, my clothes were another. Because in Adrienne's opinion I had always been underdressed, I chose what I wore with care. A solid black shirt, a white-and-black-checked cashmere coat and, for a touch of insouciance, a pair of jeans.

The tube took me to Green Park, and I strolled down Piccadilly in unseasonably warm and humid weather. Long past the age where I believed anybody, especially women, noticed me, I nevertheless hoped that the last thing I looked like was a man with an ax to grind, a grievance to settle. Amid the flotsam and jetsam that whirlpooled in my brain, there bobbed like a life preserver a single resolve. More than anything, I was determined not to act mad—in either sense of the word. The last time I encountered Adrienne, we had had frantic sex in the front seat of a car. The time before that, I had hit her. Somewhere between these extremes, there had to be a happy medium.

At the restaurant on Half Moon Street, Adrienne hadn't shown up. After removing the files, I checked my tennis bag with the maître d' and waited. When she pushed through the revolving door, I had the advantage of watching her without being seen. She had on black slacks, a green silk blouse and a scarf knotted around her neck, just like in college. A fringed pashmina draped her shoulders, as if she feared the restaurant would be air-conditioned.

When she spotted me, she appeared unsure of herself. Maybe she didn't recognize me. Then she smiled. Her face, except for frown lines on her forehead, was unmarked, her beauty preserved by good bones and expensive pampering. The gap between her front teeth had disappeared. Caps, I presumed, or some orthodontic procedure. I missed that minor flaw.

In the dining room, a glass atrium roof showed a sky full of scudding clouds and bright bars of sunlight. Adrienne motioned for me to sit beside her. "I'm not being flirtatious," she said. "I have trouble hearing."

From an old flame, this was a funny and poignant admission. Yet the truth was, she did sound flirtatious, even as she asked about my family.

"Tell me about your wife," she said.

"She's lovely and long-suffering."

"But what does she do?"

"She takes care of me. I'm very high maintenance."

"I bet you are. So's my husband. Before I left on this trip, I cooked him dinners for a month and left them in the freezer. All he has to do is microwave them. It would surprise you how competent I am in the kitchen. I remember in California I fell down in that department."

"I never felt malnourished." I set the adoption file between us.

"What won't surprise you is that my husband didn't get along with my mother any better than you did."

"There's a point in his favor."

"Are you happy?" she asked.

"At this moment?"

"Don't be a smart aleck." She nudged me with her elbow, as she might have done during one of our study dates. "Have you had a happy life?"

"The Adrienne Daly I remember claimed she didn't care about happiness. She just didn't want to lead a boring life."

"Did I say that? I don't think I'd be so quick to put down happiness these days. Tell me, though, has your life been interesting?"

"Yes, it has."

"Mine too." She shrugged the pashmina from her shoulders. The air was warm and close. She reached out a hand and laid it on my arm, rubbing the material of my jacket between her fingertips, as a sleepy child would a favorite blanket. Her eyes, along with her voice, went slightly soft-focus. "This is hard for me, Mike. I almost didn't come."

"Why?"

"I was afraid."

"Of what?"

"You. Your temper. I remember how things ended between us the last time I saw you."

"I think you're thinking of the time before that," I said.

Adrienne cocked her head at an angle and removed her hand from my arm. "I'm thinking of the time you slapped me. On the phone sometimes you've sounded cold and, I don't know, patrician . . . like you're looking down your nose."

I had to laugh. "Me? Patrician? You're the one with the frosty telephone voice. I've defended you to Amy, told her not to let it bother her."

The waiter saved Adrienne from having to speak about Amy. We ordered tea and a couple of club sandwiches. When he left, she said, "Nobody ever hit me before. Or since. Do you beat your wife?"

It was tempting to tell her that neither my wife nor anybody else had ever hurt me as badly as she had. Instead, I said there was no excuse for what I had done. To add to my shame, I had wanted to help her, but I knew there were times in LA when I had done her more harm than good. I apologized for whatever pain I had caused her.

The waiter brought our lunch, and while Adrienne poured us each a cup of tea, I confessed that I had been inexperienced and unprepared to live with her in California. "Wet behind the ears doesn't begin to describe me back then," I said. "You just happened to share your secret with someone who had as many problems as you did. You'd have to know my family to understand what I'm saying. But even if I'd been older and squared away, it never figured to be easy for us starting out together with you pregnant. I realized that when my wife was pregnant. It's a stressful time. Still, I'm sorry I didn't do a better job."

Adrienne broke off a crust of bread and a sliver of bacon from her club sandwich, and as she chewed it, I presumed she was composing an apology for the mistakes she had made. Instead, she asked, "What about your books? Are you sorry about them too?"

"I thought we settled this on the phone. I never wrote anything with the purpose of hurting you."

"Then why does every one of your horrible female characters have something of me in her?"

"This may come as a shock to you, Adrienne, but I have known other women. And I don't spend years working on a novel just to rub you the wrong way."

Still she insisted that my writing had reduced her to a caricature and demeaned everything we had done together. "You even made what we did in bed seem ugly."

I had had bad reviews in my career, but this was the worst, and I knew it was futile to debate a critic. To ease her off the subject and onto ones that interested me, I pled guilty to poor art, faulty technique and a failure of imagination. Even then, Adrienne wasn't satisfied. "Reading your books," she said, "made me wonder whether you ever loved me, whether you were the man I thought you were."

I invited her to consider the possibility that she had given me ample reason to feel the same doubts about her. I pointed out that I had apologized. If she was sorry for anything, she hadn't mentioned it.

"Why should I be sorry?" she asked. "I don't have anything to apologize for."

"Nothing at all?"

"No."

I didn't know how to respond. Or rather, any response risked destroying the slightest prospect of achieving what I was here for.

"You pushed me away," she said. "You might claim you were pushing to get married, but everything you did indicated that that was the last thing that would have worked. Can you honestly say you'd be better off now if we had stayed together?"

I shook my head. "You did me a great favor."

She caught the irony, but not the truth that underlay it. "You had a total fixation with me," she said. "That's flattering at first, but if we had married, you wouldn't have had the time and I wouldn't have had the space to accomplish anything."

"I seem to remember accomplishing things in California," I drawled. "I had a job. I took a night course. I finished a novel and applied to graduate school. And oh, yes, I found a doctor for you and an adoption agency."

To my surprise, she laid her hand back on my arm. "And we spent an awful lot of time in bed. I have lovely memories of those months."

One by one, she removed them like heirlooms from a velvet-lined chest and held them up for my admiration—her memories of seeing *Black Orpheus* and declaring that we had to travel to Brazil someday, of the restaurant where I'd first eaten snails, of the jazz club in Hermosa Beach where we'd listened to John Coltrane live, of evenings after work when we had walked to an outdoor basketball court and shot hoops by starlight.

"It was fun," she said. "Not depressing and dreary like you seem to think. I didn't inflict my sadness on you."

As Adrienne recalled our stay in California, it sounded like a sabbatical that she had orchestrated for my benefit.

"Remind me again," I said, "why you were there with me."

"Because you were cute. And when you weren't angry, you were terrific company."

"I wasn't fishing for compliments. Didn't it have something to do with a baby?"

"Of course you'd never let me forget that. Still, it wasn't as lousy a time as you make it out to be in your books. You had great raw material, but you've never described what we were for each other."

"What's that?"

"Soul mates."

She spoke so solemnly that I couldn't help smiling. "Maybe that was the problem. You wanted a soul mate. I wanted a body mate."

"I haven't forgotten the physical side to our relationship."

As she launched into an amazingly explicit account of our sex life, it struck me, just as it had when we first met, how open Adrienne could be in conversation. Despite her staid politics and stuffy social decorum, she was willing to talk about anything. This had once persuaded me that we were passionately connected. Back then, swimming in the warmth of her consoling words like an embryo in amniotic fluid, I had ignored that talk can be a kind of camouflage for the closed core of a person. It troubled me that that was what Adrienne's words might be now—a screen for what she really had in mind.

When she ended up by vowing, "There's nothing I wouldn't do for you," I said, "How about telling Amy I'm not her father? Is that too much to ask of a soul mate?"

Adrienne removed her hand from my arm. "We've been over this. You know my position. I've spent years building a wall around myself. Why would I tear it down? Why second-guess a decision I believe was the right one? It's for her own good that I gave her up—hers and everyone else's. My obligation is to my husband and our children."

"Your kids don't need to know. You said your husband already does."

"That doesn't mean he's not furious that you gave this girl our name and phone numbers. You didn't have to involve me."

"Look," I said, losing patience, "you *are* involved. You put my name on her birth certificate. How the hell was I supposed to account for that without telling her the truth?"

"Did you tell her about Dave?"

"Yes, I did."

"And you don't see anything wrong with that when we don't know who she is or what she's after?"

"It's obvious what she's after. She wants to meet her birth parents. She wants her medical history."

Adrienne tore another corner off her club sandwich. She had eaten very little and appeared to take a bite only to change the subject. "Doesn't it seem fishy," she said, "that Amy found you, not Dave or me?"

"Yeah, I *was* surprised. From information in the adoption file, it shouldn't have been hard to find you. Read it yourself."

When I held out the manila folder, she waved it away. "Know what my husband thinks? He doesn't believe Amy got a bee in her bonnet and tracked you down. He thinks you've learned investigative tricks as a journalist and used them to trace Amy. Then you filled her full of ideas about me and Dave."

"That's ridiculous."

"Actually, my husband suspects something more. He thinks maybe you hired this girl to pretend—or convinced some innocent kid to believe—that she's my daughter."

"Your husband sounds very inventive and not a little paranoid."

"You swear you didn't do it? Coach Amy and send her after me?"

"Why would I do that?"

"To hurt me because you think I hurt you."

"Look, Adrienne, if I wanted to hurt you, I wouldn't waste energy on some cockamamie scheme. I could have done it a long time ago."

"Done what?" she asked.

"Don't be disingenuous. Would you have liked to discuss Amy with Reagan or Bush or the *Washington Post* or some Senate oversight committee that was reviewing your security clearance?"

"Are you suggesting that having a baby before I was married disqualifies me from public service?"

"Not for a second. If the story ever came out, I bet most people would sympathize. Even your kids would be thrilled to hear that their mother is human."

"I have no interest in finding out," she said. "I have no interest in starring on the *Oprah Winfrey Show*."

"That's what I assumed. You're not the type to air her laundry in public. So that's why I never put you in that position. But I didn't think you'd mind talking to Amy privately and setting her straight about me."

"Now who's being disingenuous? You let a complete stranger into my life. How do you know she's not after my money?"

"How do you know she's not after mine?"

"Do you have any?"

"As a matter of fact, I do. Not that I'll have much left after my sons finish college."

"Where do they go?"

"The older one went to Princeton. The younger one starts there next year."

"Princeton!" she exclaimed. "Well, what do you know about that? The poor boy with the giant chip on his shoulder is rich. If we met now, maybe you wouldn't be so prickly and defensive. Listening to you, looking at you, I have trouble believing you're the same man."

"Three decades will do that," I said.

"No, you look very distinguished. You look like a Republican congressman."

"My bank balance has changed, not my mind."

For no apparent reason—unless the mention of money prompted a memory of my 1964 Christmas splurge—Adrienne brought up the suede slacks I had given her. "I still have them. Every time I pack or unpack, I come across them in the closet. I have no idea whether they fit me now. But I'd never throw them away. Whenever I move houses—and think how many times that's been—I always bring them along."

We spent the next couple of hours in this fashion—alternately chewing over the past and chewing out each other. Neither of us had much success at sticking to a subject, and as we zigzagged from nasty accusations to nostalgic reminiscences, the sky above the atrium changed as mercurially as the conversation. A breezy summer day boiled up into a gray blustery winter afternoon, followed by a brief interval of autumnal sunlight, then a dramatic spring downpour. While rain drummed at the glass, I excused myself to call my tennis partner and cancel our match. I figured this was a chance for Adrienne to sneak a glance at the adoption file.

When I got back, the manila folder lay where it had been, and I couldn't tell whether she had opened it. But something had etched a frown on her face, deepening the lines on her forehead.

"The tea's cold," I said. "How about some wine?"

She nodded, and the waiter cleared away our uneaten lunch and poured us a couple of glasses of dry white wine. Adrienne sipped hers and said as if anxious to have it on the record, "You know, I never asked you to come to California with me."

"My memory is that I offered and you accepted. Can we agree that it was mutual?"

"Not if you assume I told you I was pregnant because I was begging for help."

"I've learned not to assume anything about you, Adrienne. But I have wondered why you told me."

"Because I loved you and didn't want to lie to you."

"And why did you tell Dave?"

"Because I thought he had a right to know."

"And the third man?" I asked.

"What third man?"

"The one that's mentioned in the file. You told Mrs. Christian you had three marriage proposals when you were pregnant."

"Oh, you mean Roger. My drama professor, my mentor. He'd have done anything for me."

"Weren't you lucky to have three fellows clamoring to help?"

She set down her wine glass. "I don't know how serious Roger was about marrying me. He was much older. But he promised he'd pay for an abortion if that's what I wanted."

"I'm surprised you never mentioned him to me."

"I figured you'd cross-examine me like you're doing now."

"It's hard for me to imagine a man offering to marry you or pay for an abortion unless something else was going on."

Adrienne bridled. Color flooded her cheeks. "What are you hinting at?"

"I'm not hinting at anything. I'm asking outright. Is Roger Amy's father? Is that why you won't talk to her? Because you'd have to admit that you lied about Dave?"

"What an awful thing to say. You make me sound like a tramp. You stayed with me. You were willing to marry me before you had sex with me. Why wouldn't Roger do the same?"

"Soul mates," I said ruefully. "I guess they do that sort of thing."

"Exactly." She signaled to the waiter for more wine. "No matter what you say, Mike, I refuse to play the role of the fallen woman and make some melodramatic confession. Maybe because you're Catholic, you believe in pleading for forgiveness, but I've moved on. I wish you would too."

"It's tough to move on when I have questions about the past."

"Oh, Christ, what more?"

"Why's my name on Amy's birth certificate?"

"That's no big mystery. Mewshaw is the name we used from the start at the Children's Home Society."

"But they knew we weren't married and I wasn't the father. Why didn't Mrs. Christian insist that you use your own name?"

"Why's it so important? I wanted Mewshaw on the birth certificate as a tribute to you because you played such an important role in the baby's birth."

"It never occurred to you that that might cause problems for me?"

"I didn't think anybody would ever see it. Mrs. Christian swore the whole case history, including the birth certificate, would be sealed. I resent it that the rules changed after the fact and without my knowledge or permission. My husband's as angry as I am. He's considering legal action for invasion of privacy."

"Before you do that, maybe you ought to have a look at the file."

This time, I didn't wait for her to take it. I dropped the folder onto her lap and left the table to phone Linda and explain that I would be late for dinner. But if I expected the "nonidentifying information" to shake Adrienne's self-possession, I was sorely mistaken. When I returned, she sat with the sheaf of papers on her knees, her expression bland and unblinking. Here was a lady well practiced in the diplomatic arts. With such sangfroid, she would never tip her hand in negotiations.

I flicked a finger at the snapshot of Amy attached by a paper clip to the first page. "What do you think?"

"I don't see any resemblance."

"You're joking."

"As in so many cases, Mike, you're seeing what you prefer to see."

"I'd say you're refusing to recognize what you don't care to admit."

"As for the rest of this—" she rattled the pages—"I question whether it's legal. It certainly isn't ethical. I believed that my counseling sessions were confidential and that a patient-caregiver privilege applied."

"The Children's Home Society maintains that California law allows them to release this kind of information."

"But they take everything out of context, and there's all this editorializing. That business about the Miss Maryland pageant, maybe to Mrs. Christian it was important, but I assure you it's not on my CV."

"That's a shame," I said. "I bet the State Department has never had another woman with your credentials."

This coaxed a smile from her. She poured half of her wine into my glass.

"What I've always wondered," I said, "is when you made up your mind what you intended to do after the baby was born? Did it dawn on you gradually? Or did you decide early on that I played no part in your plans?"

"I hate to hear you talk like that, Mike." She mimed covering her ears. "I can't imagine how it must be to live with such low self-esteem. Right up until the end, even after you hit me, I loved you and hoped things would work out."

"Work out how?"

"Oh, that we'd meet again in our thirties and take up where we left off."

"Really?" I flipped the pages in her lap and pointed to the last two sentences, which read, "Your mother was quite sure what she wanted to do with her life. She did plan to go to Europe with her grandmother, your great-grandmother, after returning home."

Adrienne didn't flinch. "If there's one thing I never knew back then, it's what I'd do next. I had trouble enough living day to day."

"So it's pure coincidence—" I spoke in a voice as flat and uninflected as hers—"that after we came back from LA, that's what you did? Moved down to your grandmother's place in Miami, then traveled around the world with her, just like it says you planned to do?"

"There was never a plan," she said. "It just worked out that way."

I realized I could keep grinding at this with her for the rest of my life and never hit bottom. She recognized it herself and reminded me of the film, *Rashomon,* that had been her touchstone for decades. Truth, she said, depends on your point of view.

I lifted the pages off Adrienne's lap. "I wish you'd leave them with me," she said.

"I wouldn't think you'd want them."

"But I do."

"I'll send you a copy," I said.

"I'd rather not have them show up in the mail at my house."

"There's a Xerox place around the corner. We'll have them photo-copied."

"What about the picture of Amy? Can I keep it?"

"It's the only one I've got. And didn't you claim there's no resemblance?"

"Please, Mike."

I placed it in her hand, the last card I had to play. "Sure, she belongs to you." I could only hope that someday she'd look at it and change her mind and contact her daughter.

While we were copying the documents, Adrienne said, "Promise me you'll never write about this."

"Sorry, I can't do that."

"Why not?"

"You have your ways of coping. I have mine."

"I don't follow."

"You have a painful experience and you build a wall around it. I respect your decision, even if I disagree with it. But for me, the only thing that helps is putting things down on paper."

"Fine. Write about Amy and leave me out of it."

"But you're the heart of the story."

Once we'd finished, we stepped out into the rain and walked a few blocks down Piccadilly toward Hyde Park. Huddling under my umbrella, holding on to my elbow, Adrienne seemed exhilarated, perhaps because the questions had stopped. She was headed for Knightsbridge to meet friends and asked if I'd like to go that far with her. I told her I was going in the opposite direction. I air-kissed her cheeks, promised we'd do this again in thirty years and bundled her into a black cab.

CHAPTER EIGHTEEN

G od knows why Adrienne choreographed that get-together in London. Certainly not for the pleasure of my company—although maybe she was mildly curious to see how I had aged. Whatever she came away with, besides Amy's file and her photograph, I doubted it was a sense of closure. Or was I only speaking for myself? I came away feeling wide open, knowing that nothing had been resolved.

When Amy heard that I had given Adrienne her picture, she sent me a replacement. A snapshot from her wedding day, it showed her in a full-length white gown and her husband in a tuxedo, the two of them on a hillside overlooking the sprawl of the San Fernando Valley. She appeared to be just as happy as she always sounded over the telephone. But she admitted to me that she felt let down by her birth mother.

Meanwhile, her search for Dave had been unsuccessful. Amy didn't say how she had gone about looking for him, and I didn't ask. It didn't seem as if she should have had much trouble locating him. But perhaps after the disappointment with Adrienne, she feared another rejection and hadn't tried very hard. I took that as a reason—or was it an excuse?—not to extend my help; I didn't care to have her get hurt again.

Only as the months passed did it spring to mind that my motives might not be so noble. For all my concern about Amy, I couldn't deny an element of selfishness. Arrogating to myself the role of father-surrogate, did I fear being supplanted by the real one? That unflattering thought was enough to goad me into action.

This time I didn't require Lexis-Nexis, Google or any other search engine. I called the University of Maryland alumni office, which had Dave's address and phone number on record. Although they wouldn't furnish this information without his permission, they agreed to relay a message and let him contact me if he cared to.

The message demanded tact as well as guile. My name might mean nothing to Dave after all these years. On the other hand, if he did remember me, he might be disinclined to call back. He had his reasons to hate me, just as I thought I had good cause to feel antipathy toward him. In the end I informed the alumni office that I was a friend of Adrienne Daly's and had news of her that pertained to Dave.

He phoned the next day. The owner of a realty company in Florida, he had an affable manner, friendly, polite, almost courtly. He addressed me as "Sir," and it was difficult to visualize him as a high-pressure salesman. He sounded like he would acknowledge it if a house had termites or a leaky basement.

I proceeded slowly, cautiously, explaining that I had known Adrienne at the University of Maryland, then out in California. Was he aware that she had had a baby in 1964?

"Yessir," Dave said.

"I'm in touch with a person who claims to be Adrienne's child."

"Boy or girl?" he asked.

"A girl."

"That's great. I've always wondered."

As I inched along, tentatively posing questions, Dave interrupted to say that while he appreciated my discretion, I needn't bother soft-pedaling the subject. "I'm the father. At least, Adrienne told me I was. What's my daughter's name?"

"Amy."

"I'd like to talk to her. Meet her."

"I'll tell her that and pass along your number, if you don't mind."

"Hell, no, I don't mind. I'd be delighted to hear from her. Does Adrienne know about Amy? Have the two of them spoken?"

"Yes, briefly. It didn't go well. Adrienne promised to call her back but never has. I'd like to be sure how you feel before I talk to Amy. She doesn't deserve another rejection."

"Jesus, of course I won't reject her. I can't believe that about Adrienne. Are you in contact with her?" Dave asked.

"I've spoken to her a few times, and I had lunch with her."

"I'd like to speak to her myself. It's been years. Do you have her number?"

"I'd rather not be the source of that. She was pretty perturbed that I gave it to Amy. I hope you understand."

"Yessir, I do."

"She's not that hard to find."

"It's probably a bad idea. There's never been any sign that she'd like to hear from me."

"Well, she's married and has two more kids. I suppose she has to think of them first."

"I've got a boy myself," Dave said. "He's seventeen. He'll be happy to hear he has a half-sister. He'll be happy for me. But I understand what you're saying about Adrienne. Where for me it's a joy to finally meet

Amy, for Adrienne it's a nightmare. She was always smart and capable, and she had political ambitions."

I told Dave that she had realized those ambitions, and I supplied a short summary of her career.

"Doesn't surprise me a bit," he said. "Her parents had these grandiose expectations of her. When she got pregnant, that wasn't part of the plan. I wasn't part of the plan either. She had an agenda, and as a good conservative Republican, she couldn't have any skeletons, such as an illegitimate baby, in her closet."

Dave added that he was a Republican himself, locally active, and he wanted me to be aware that he bore Adrienne no ill will. Far from it, he cherished his memories of her. "My only mistake was thinking I could make her love me. I can unequivocally state she's the one woman I flat-out loved. I would have slit my wrists for her. I've never reached the same intensity of emotion since. She definitely left a mark on me. She left scars."

I was beginning to feel acutely uncomfortable as he unburdened the secrets of his heart. My natural instinct was to sympathize, even identify, with him. Yet this was the man who, in Adrienne's telling, had pressured her into sex and gotten her pregnant on purpose. I cut him short, promised I'd call Amy as soon as I hung up and couldn't help wishing him well with his daughter.

"Thank you, sir," he said.

When I phoned Amy that her birth father was waiting to hear from her, she was ebullient. "I can't thank you enough. This is the best birthday gift I could ask for."

A few days later, she turned thirty-three, and at last I thought I could turn the page on that chapter of my life. The irony was that while Adrienne, my soul mate, refused to tell Amy I wasn't her father, Dave, from whom I had expected animosity, did me the favor. In answer to Amy's call, he sent her a letter on business stationery festooned with a palm tree and spiked with exclamation points.

Dear Amy:

Thought I would use the computer (spell check) and just type for a few days and see what comes out!

Let's see, I was born Feb. 26th, 1937 in San Antonio, TX. Your Grandfather, my dad, was a General in the Air Force. I moved all over the world growing up!! Pop married your Grandmother in 1932 after he graduated from West Point.

Dad had the 85th Division at Andrew's Air Force Base outside of (Washington) D.C. at the time I was to go to college so I went to the University of Maryland. Had two years there, did poorly, Dad threw me in the Army for two years, got out, went back and graduated!

While still at the University, joined a Fraternity, across the street from the Sorority where I met your Mother, Adrienne Daly. I went with her for two years. I thought we were happy, I certainly was! I gave her my Fraternity Pin. (The thing to do back then!)

When Adrienne became pregnant, decided not to marry me and go to California to give up the child, you, I was devastated but there was nothing I could do!! She was, and is a very strong person, very directed and goal oriented!

She had other plans and I was not part of them. Anyway, she came back in Jan. 1965 for a very short time and then moved to NY City to work. I tried to see her while she was in D.C. and up there, even flying up with the hope she would see me but she would not!! I understand that she married into a famous family and became very active in Republican Party Politics and became

Assistant Secretary of State for Reagan and Bush's administrations. From the material I've enclosed you can see that we were both very active politically!

I worked for several Republican candidates and have ended up as a town commissioner for the past twelve years.

After 1965 (it was a very bad year) I worked for a wholly owned subsidiary of Dun & Bradstreet for twenty years. Got married in 1970 for one year, long story, maybe later!! Got married the second time in 1979. Had one son, picture enclosed! By the way, he says, "Hi Sister"!!! He is looking forward to meeting you! My Sister, picture enclosed also, says "hi" and is also looking forward to meeting you. She remembers Adrienne very well and thought I had bitten off more than I could chew back in 1963. At any rate, in 1993 I got divorced for the second time and David is living with me!!! Vanity is a terrible thing, I had to name him after me!!! He is a senior in high school and I am about to strangle your brother. His grades are not the best so we are looking forward to a two-year junior college, a little growing up, and hopefully two more years at the University!!

Amy, I have been doing a lot of thinking about your Mother's reaction when you called her up. I realize it must have hurt you at the time but having known your Mother as well as I did I think I know what she was "thinking." Her whole life has been politics, and a conservative Republican to boot! Any scandal i.e., an unwed Mother, would kill her politically. I have little doubt that Adrienne will probably run for the House of Representatives. Adrienne and I worked very hard to get her Mother elected to the Maryland State House. We were successful! I feel in the future Adrienne will want to see you. Michael said that when he saw her in London she took a picture of you with her!!

Amy, gotta go!! Want to get this in the mail. I have put together a few pictures that you might find interesting!
Love, your Dad

Among the photos Dave sent were two that looked like black-and-white snapshots from a college yearbook. One showed Dave, dressed in a dark suit, white shirt and tie, grinning face-forward at the camera. He must have been in his mid-twenties, but a receding hairline gave him the look of a slightly older man, a tanned, happy guy in his early thirties. Adrienne, who couldn't have been more than twenty-one, also looked older and more sophisticated than a college senior. In three-quarter profile, lips slightly parted, her dark hair done up in a chignon, she might have been a model—not a gaunt high-fashion mannequin, but a healthy, attractive woman in an ad for skin cleanser or shampoo.

When Amy received the pictures, it struck her again how much she resembled her birth mother. But Dave's snapshot didn't set off the same vibrations. Just as she had done with the newspaper photos of Adrienne, she examined Dave's picture feature by feature. She laid a finger over his nose and mouth and studied the shape of his eyes. She moved the finger around his face, isolating his jawline, his forehead, his ears. Nothing reminded her of herself. Nothing provoked a visceral response that validated him as her father.

Still, she accepted his word. What choice did she have? His account matched the information from the Children's Home Society file and was consistent with what I had told her. She was grateful for the warmth and openness of his letters and the flowers he sent every Christmas Eve for her birthday, unfailingly signed "Love, Your Dad." But she didn't jump on a plane and fly off to Florida to meet him. Nor did Dave travel to Los Angeles for a reunion. Each appeared reluctant to seize the initiative. As Amy confided to me, after Adrienne's rebuff, she was wary of imposing herself on anybody. "I'm not looking for another family," she said again.

Her own family had started to grow. She and her husband had a son, then several years later they had a second boy. Her husband's business flourished, and Amy enjoyed being a full-time stay-at-home mom. They vacationed with the kids in Hawaii, in the Canadian Rockies on ski holidays, in Miami for the Orange Bowl, but they didn't cross the state to the Gulf Coast to visit Dave.

This surprised me, but it shouldn't have. After all, I knew what it was to drop in on a father whose reaction was that of a stranger. As I aged, I knew what it was to confront a man who had my white hair, my eyes, my pale Irish complexion, the same range of scowling expressions, and yet to feel no affinity. When my father was over eighty and I was still eager to bridge the gulf between us, I tried to hug him, only to have him draw back and ask what the hell I was doing. In the last decade of his life, I saw him just once. We had dinner, fittingly enough, at a fish restaurant in the Nevada desert.

So no, it shouldn't have surprised me that Amy and Dave hadn't gotten together. Still, it saddened me. And when I mentioned this to Amy's adoptive mother, she acknowledged that Amy had lingering doubts whether Dave was her father.

That Dave might harbor some of the same doubts might explain why he hadn't made the first move. Once deceived and left to feel like a fool, any man could be forgiven for not opening himself up to that again.

I began ruminating more and more about Dave. Or rather, since I knew next to nothing about him, I found myself speculating. It interested me that his letter to Amy revealed that he was raising his son by his second marriage. He sounded like a solid citizen—town commissioner, self-employed businessman, single father, someone who owned up to past mistakes and wasn't afraid to discuss his feelings. The man bore little resemblance to the one Adrienne had described to me.

So much of what I believed about the past depended on what she had said. And I had repeated it to Amy as though it were gospel. Yet all I could swear to was, as legal eagles express it, what I knew of my own knowledge, what I had done and witnessed firsthand—which added up to small fragments of the full mosaic. To give Amy the whole story, to understand it myself and to be fair to Dave, I needed to know his side.

Still in the Tampa area selling real estate, he didn't recognize my name when I rang him. I had to cue him that we had spoken several years before when I had called to tell him about Amy.

"Oh, yessir! What can I do for you?"

For a few minutes we gabbed about what a lovely woman his daughter was, and how much happiness he got from the photographs of his grandsons. "I should be shot," Dave said, "for not flying out to visit them and Amy. But I will one of these days."

In Florida, spending the winter in Key West with my wife to escape the damp cold of London, I said I'd like to meet him. I said I was thinking of doing a book about Amy's adoption and the events surrounding it.

Dave's response, one that a writer rarely hears, was instant enthusiasm. "That's a terrific idea. I'd like to meet you too. Let me know when you're coming."

"I'll probably ask a lot of questions," I said. "But if you feel like I'm sticking my nose in the wrong place, just tell me to back off, and I will."

"Hell," he said, laughing, "I'm sixty-seven years old and we're talking about something that started in a 1956 Ford convertible. You can ask me anything."

When I phoned with my plane schedule and inquired about hotels in his neighborhood, Dave said, "I'll pick you up at the airport. Forget about a hotel. You can stay at my place. I've got plenty of room."

"That's nice of you, but I'll catch a cab. I don't want to impose on you."

"It's no trouble. I'll be in a white Lexus sedan. What do you look like?"

Again I protested, but Dave said, "You're really going to piss me off if you don't stay here. Now, lemme throw someone on the line, an old friend of mine from Maryland who's in town for a few days. He knew Adrienne, and you might have some questions for him."

"Does he know about Amy?"

"Of course; I told him. I've told all my friends."

"And he knows Adrienne's her birth mother?"

"Absolutely. He knew from the get-go that she was pregnant. I did a lot of crying on his shoulder when she dumped me."

A guy named Joe came on the line, and he was every bit as gregarious as Dave. He didn't actually have much to say about Adrienne except that she had been a very focused college girl, driven to succeed, and that she had led Dave around like a puppy dog. In the background, Dave squawked and playfully protested.

"He's a great guy," Joe said. "Tell you what kind of fella Dave is. Back in the day, we were driving in his brand-new 1966 Mustang and somehow I acted up and dented the dashboard. Any other man would have been mad as hell. But not Dave. He forgave me on the spot. That's how he is, very friendly and forgiving."

Was this code? I wondered. Was Joe implying that Dave had forgiven me? Or was it Adrienne he had forgiven?

When Joe handed the phone back to Dave, he asked if I had any recent pictures of Adrienne. He hadn't seen her since she was twenty-one, and he was eager to take a look at her now. I told him I had some newspaper articles, and a few of these had grainy photographs.

"Be sure to bring them," he said. "I'll be waiting at the arrival area."

.   .   .

The morning I flew out, Linda said, "Careful. Maybe he means to sucker you into his house and smother you in your sleep."

Wisecracks notwithstanding, there was something to what she said. I had long regarded Dave as a competitor, if not an outright enemy—the man who had knocked up my girlfriend. And I supposed that he viewed me as the fellow who had shouldered him aside. In our day, that had been a fighting offense, an ignominy not to be forgotten or forgiven. Yet he acted as easygoing about the past as about everything else.

At the Tampa airport, Dave wore Bermuda shorts, a polo shirt and Topsiders with no socks. A big-boned, fleshy fellow with a bald sunburned pate, he greeted me with a broad smile and an energetic handshake. It might have been the same geniality he accorded prospective house buyers, but since he had nothing to sell me, his warmth seemed genuine.

At midday, the road was empty and we sped off from the city, across bridges and causeways to a waterfront community. Sun dazzled the bay, and a breeze swept the marina, strong enough to rock sailboats and set their riggings chiming against aluminum masts. From the airport arrival area to Dave's front porch, the trip took forty-five minutes, and I can't decide what impressed me more—that he was willing to drive such a distance to chauffeur me or that we never once fell silent. We talked about marriage, children, careers, aging, health, death.

House proud, Dave escorted me around his place, a ranch-style home built on a finger of land that had been dredged up out of Bocaciega Bay. From his front window, we had a view of pleasure craft skimming the bay, creating little more disturbance than water bugs on a pond. Dave's boat was up on davits at his own dock. As we crossed the lawn to look at it, thick, spongy St. Augustine grass squelched under my feet. He conceded that he seldom used the boat these days and was thinking of selling it but hated to let it go.

That appeared to be a constant theme with him—hating to let go. The house had been his father's retirement home. The general had had it built for less than $30,000. Now, as Dave knew from his real estate buisness, it was worth close to a million. But he wasn't tempted to list it on the market and cash in. He meant to hold on.

Why should he sell? His son, now in his twenties, lived nearby, and Dave's third wife, Paulette, had a teaching job in the next county. The commute was too brutal to make every day, so she kept a condo near the school and came home on weekends. With a wink, he confessed that sometimes he got lonely and drove up to be with her. But tonight wouldn't be one of those nights. The two of us would be baching it, with him in the master bedroom at one end of the sprawling house and me at the other end, in a bedroom decorated in bright tropical colors. Atop the chest of drawers in the guest room wedding photos featured Dave and Paulette, a tall, attractive blond years his junior.

Between the two bedrooms, the intervening space—a dining area, a seating alcove, a Florida room with picture windows and skylights— didn't appear to be lived in. Dave spent most of his time in a room that had been renovated into a combination office and den. While one corner of it was all business, with a desk, file drawers, computer and fax machine, the rest was devoted to entertainment. In addition to a flat-screen television, there was a professional-looking telescope that seemed capable of scanning the galaxy. On the walls hung Dave's framed undergraduate degree, a group portrait of his fraternity, a class photo from high school and a collage fashioned out of his father's medals and field decorations and his spurs from West Point.

As we settled into a couple of padded leather chairs, we might have been in the lounge of the Bachelor Officer's Quarters, chatting about old campaigns. A tiny fluffy dog, a Lhasa apso named Killer, stayed with us, watching me warily and occasionally barking and dashing to the front door when it heard a passerby. Dave said, "Killer's all bark and no bite."

In his amiable, self-deprecating manner, Dave seemed determined to prove that he had neither a bark nor a bite. For a writer, conversations with sources can often be as painful as pulling teeth. But interviewing Dave was as effortless as prying fruit out of a Jell-O mold. Half the time, I didn't need to ask questions. He volunteered answers.

When I handed him the newspaper photos of Adrienne, he marveled at how beautiful she was, how much she still resembled the girl he had loved. Then he read the articles and marveled at how much she had achieved. His pride in her was undiminished after four decades. As he acknowledged, she had always run the show, and in his opinion the show had been stunningly first class.

Not that he hailed from humble origins. In his family, there were five generals. Dave had been expected to follow the military tradition. After high school he had started off at Texas A&M but hated life as an Aggie and a cadet, and his father had permitted him to transfer to the University of Maryland. When he didn't keep his grades up, the general put through a call to the Pentagon and ordered his son drafted. "You couldn't do that today," Dave said, "but that's how it worked then—the old-boy network—and it was the best thing for me."

After the army, he reenrolled at the University of Maryland as a veteran, a man among college kids, a fellow with a certain amount of savoir faire, not to mention money. When his fraternity invited the sorority girls across the street over for a community sing, he spotted Adrienne Daly as they gathered around the piano and fell in love at first sight. "It was instantaneous," Dave said. They started dating, but because he respected her, because he sensed she was "a keeper," he didn't rush her. They went out together for six months before they had sex.

"The funny thing was," Dave said, "the first time we had intercourse, she forgot and left her underpants in my car. I took them to her at her sorority house the next morning."

"Could we slow down a minute?" I asked. In a thirty-year career of interviewing cops, criminals, convicted killers, athletes, movie stars and writers, I can't remember ever before interrupting somebody once he was in free flow. With Dave, however, I felt ill at ease and wondered whether he would regret what he was revealing. But he behaved as if he had been waiting half his life to discuss Adrienne Daly.

He said they were sexually involved "all during her junior and senior years. We'd drive up US1 and check into a motel for a few hours. Later on, I had my own apartment. I've forgotten a lot of things in my life, but not that. I remember she liked to be on top."

Adrienne had told Mrs. Christian—she had maintained the same to me—that Dave had pressured her into sex and made her pregnant on purpose to force her to marry him. But this didn't fit his recollection of their long-running affair. "I didn't force her, and she never refused me." He popped a piece of Nicorette gum into his mouth and chewed vigorously as he spoke. "She never even said no, it's the wrong time of the month."

"What did you use for birth control? Adrienne said you claimed to be on an experimental oral male contraceptive."

Dave screwed his face into an expression of comic incredulity, then burst into laughter so loud that Killer barked. "We never used anything. We just went ahead and did it. I can see where she might say it was intentional on my part because the way I felt, if she gets pregnant, that's great. We'll get married. If not, that's okay too. I loved her and thought we'd get married whatever happened." He laughed again. "Stupid me."

"You say you were involved with Adrienne all during her senior year, but by March she was pregnant." I didn't add that by then she and I had been dating for months and had discussed marriage.

"Yeah, it happened one weekend when we flew to New York for a play. She didn't find out she was pregnant until late April, when she started having morning sickness. I offered to drive her to the doctor's. She said no, she'd do it on her own."

"So you were involved with her up until—"

"Right up till the day she told me the test was positive."

Stupid me, I might have echoed Dave. Far from a spur-of-the-moment trip—on which Adrienne had implied that Dave had butted in—the weekend in New York had been a long-planned romantic getaway. What's more, Adrienne had handled the logistics.

"Drama was her thing," Dave said. "I had never been to a Broadway play. Adrienne's the one who reserved tickets to *Oliver*. We sat in the fifth row center, the best seats in the house, according to her. Believe me, it was an expensive weekend. We stayed at the Waldorf Astoria. We ate at the Four Seasons. But I was out of school then and making good money, and I thought it was worth it. We had a fabulous time."

Now might have been my turn to laugh. Not at Dave, but at the sheer absurdity of their pricey escapade compared to the cokes and hamburgers I had bought her back then.

I asked how he could be sure she had gotten pregnant that particular weekend.

"Well," he said, "she swore it was then. And when I looked at the calendar, it added up."

"Adrienne said a lot of things that weren't true," I reminded him, and mentioned that in the adoption file she referred to another man.

Dave jawed at the Nicorette gum, pondering this. He didn't appear to be angry or upset, just perplexed. "Who's the other guy?"

"A former professor of hers."

"Oh, him. I know who you mean. She introduced us one day on campus. I can't believe she ever had sex with him. He was chubby and ugly and about twenty years older. Besides, to the best of my recollection, she was a virgin. I don't mean there was blood the first time, but I remember discomfort on her part, and I don't think she was faking it.

"What else was in the files?" he asked. "Anything that says how she made up her mind about me?"

I felt on the spot. He might have already received the files from Amy and been testing whether I would level with him. "She seemed to think you lacked spontaneity," I said.

Dave's measured response made me suspect that he was joking, that he meant to demonstrate just how humorously unspontaneous he could be. But he took the charge to heart. "If you're saying I like to be organized and plan ahead, then I guess I'm not spontaneous. Is that a bad thing?"

His cell phone rang. "Excuse me, sir." He spat out his gum and took a call from a client. His voice, his posture, his entire demeanor altered. No longer a man mulling over the past, he slipped into his identity as a real estate broker, a businessman hashing over mortgage rates, closing costs and tax consequences. During the two days we would spend together, I witnessed this metamorphosis a dozen times, and although the abruptness of it caught me off guard at first, I admired his ability to deal with different claims on his attention. His shift from the emotional to the practical, his refusal to palm off me or his customers with easy answers, made me like him all the more. Whatever else he might be, Dave seemed the classic American "good guy," easygoing and uncomplicated.

His honesty prompted an admission that even though he was six years Adrienne's senior, he had been naïve and immature at the age of twenty-seven. "There was so much I didn't understand. I blame it on being blinded by love or just plain dumb. She was always much smarter."

"She was also a lot less straightforward than you," I said.

"I guess." Still, he hesitated to find fault with her, and he refused to see himself as wronged. As he recounted their last meeting, he spoke with sadness, not bitterness. "We were out at her grandmother's farm. Do you know the place?"

I told him that I did.

"Imagine what a property like that, in that location, would be worth today," he said.

My lasting impression was of the nearby junkyard, but I deferred to Dave on real estate matters and urged him to go on.

"We took a walk in the fields so her grandmother wouldn't hear us," he said. "When Adrienne told me she was pregnant, I wasn't surprised, not after how sick to her stomach she had been. Then she told me she didn't want to marry me. She didn't say she didn't love me, just that she didn't want to marry me. And I felt sick myself."

"Did she say why?"

"She said she was too young, and she had a lot she planned to do with her life."

I waited for Dave to mention me, to say that Adrienne had told him she loved me. When he didn't, I thought there were limits to what even someone as self-effacing as he would confess.

"Weren't you mad at her?" I asked. "What did you say to her?"

"I was pretty upset. I can't remember saying much of anything."

"Did you see her again? Didn't you try to talk her out of it?"

"No. She made it clear there was no chance of that, and she didn't want any further contact. But then she wrote me from California. She wrote me a couple of times. She asked for my blood type and so forth.

The second letter was a lot more emotional. She said she could feel the baby moving inside her. That did make me mad. That was my baby, and she was about to give it away. I wrote back begging her to reconsider and let me keep the baby. But she never answered."

"Were you serious? Would you have raised Amy?"

"Why not? I had the money. I made thirteen thousand dollars in '65. That's more than my father was making as a general. I could have supported her."

"Yeah, but bringing up a daughter as a single father—"

"I raised my son on my own. I could have done it. When I learned that Amy's adopted mother brought her up alone and that she didn't have much money, it made me feel awful. I wish I could have helped them out and given her opportunities. When Amy and I reconnected, I wanted her to understand that I had loved Adrienne. I didn't want her to think her birth was the result of a fling or a one-night stand. I didn't run out on Adrienne and abandon her."

"Did you have any contact with Adrienne after she came back from California?"

"I tried." Dave was working on a fresh wad of Nicorette. "I called her at her family's house and left messages. She never phoned back. Then she moved to New York, and I decided I couldn't sit around and wait. I hopped on the shuttle to La Guardia and went to the Waldorf, where we spent that weekend. I left her a message that I was in town and wanted to see her. I said I'd be in the lobby all that evening. I sat there dressed in my coat and tie. She never showed up. So I caught the shuttle back to Washington. After that, I knew it was over, finished! All I did then was dream about her. Honest to God, I dreamed about her until I was in my fifties."

"Jesus, Dave, I'm sorry."

He shrugged. "I made a pain in the ass of myself whining to friends. And I lost a lot of weight, down to a hundred and sixty pounds from one ninety. I thought I had nobody to blame but myself. I thought I hadn't measured up and wasn't the man Adrienne deserved. But hey," he exclaimed, blurting the American male's signal for switching emotional gears, "she was a beautiful woman, and I had two and a half years with her that were flat-out wonderful."

Although that might have rounded off the story, Dave conceded that it hadn't ended there. In addition to dreaming about Adrienne, he had attempted to keep track of her. From time to time in Republican circles, at fund-raisers and campaign meetings, he bumped into her mother. "But Mrs. Daly was very cold to me," he said. "She kept her distance and didn't speak. Hell, she was remote with her own children and always put herself and her career first. So why should I have expected her to have any interest in me?"

He found a more receptive relative of Adrienne's, an uncle who was a dentist. For years, Dave scheduled regular appointments with the man to have his teeth cleaned. Although the dentist had no idea what had ended their romance, he remembered them as a couple in college and made it a point to provide about Adrienne's marriage and children.

But of course the uncle could tell him nothing about his baby, and Dave was reduced again to the solace of dreams. Or at times the desolation of nightmares. He feared the child had died. In crowds he found himself searching for a face that resembled his or that reminded him of Adrienne's. He played out punishing fantasies that he had failed his baby, just as he had failed Adrienne, just as he had failed in his first two marriages. "The experience with Adrienne made me leerier of women," he said, "more cynical, less willing to commit. That's my great fault, lack of commitment."

Daunted by his candor, I wondered what my own worst fault was. Dave's professed cynicism and distrust seemed nothing compared to mine. Yet maybe my greatest sin was pride. I had viewed myself as the central character, the wronged party in this affair. But meeting Amy had forced me to reconsider, and now, with Dave, I questioned whether I ever figured in the equation.

When I asked him what Adrienne had said about me, he was sitting with Killer in his lap, petting the high-strung little dog. He spoke quietly, as if gentling me as well. "I don't mean to insult you, Mike, but she never mentioned you at all."

"When I first phoned you, who did you think I was?"

"You said you were Adrienne's friend and had news about her. That was good enough for me."

"Wait a minute. I told you I was in California with her. Didn't you wonder why I was there?"

"I assumed she needed someone to help her out."

"I was more than a friend, Dave. I loved her. She said she loved me. We were engaged. I offered to raise Amy as my own child."

"I'll be damned."

"She never told you any of this?"

He shook his head. "No sir."

"She told me she didn't marry you because she was in love with me."

Dave's thick neck appeared to lose strength, and his head drooped. I was afraid that he had broken into tears. But he was laughing. What could I do but laugh along with him?

"This is crazy," he said. "I'll admit she made a fool of me, but I didn't have any idea I was *this* oblivious to what was going on. I never guessed there was another guy."

"We met once. Don't you remember? It was after a play."

"If you say it happened, it must have. But honestly, Mike, I didn't believe I had any competition. That's why it was such a shock when she said we were through and cut me loose. I wouldn't have felt so bad if I thought I lost out to somebody else. That's a hell of a lot better than thinking she dropped me for no reason. To feel like she was giving up our baby just because she didn't want to be with me . . . well, that was damn painful. But I guess you got dumped yourself. What happened?"

With the tables turned and Dave digging for answers, I offered an abridged version of events. This wasn't to hide anything from him. I was just anxious to get back to asking him about things I didn't know. But with his real estate broker's finicky attention to small print, he wasn't satisfied until he understood the bottom line.

"Why did she tell you she was pregnant if she didn't intend to marry you?" he asked.

"She said she didn't want to lie to me. She mentioned an abortion. But I told her she didn't need me for that, and she changed her mind."

"I don't believe it," he said. "Adrienne Daly would never have had an abortion. Conservative Republicans with political aspirations didn't do that, not back when it was illegal. It was more like her to move to California with you."

"Actually, we didn't move together. She left for the Republican convention in San Francisco, and I caught up with her in LA. I had to stay behind to finish summer school and save some money."

"For what?"

"Living expenses. Medical bills."

"You paid for that?"

"Most of it. Adrienne couldn't work once she started to show."

"Why didn't she use her own money? She had that new T-bird. She wasn't broke. If she didn't have the cash, she could have tapped her family."

"That was the point of going to LA. To keep it secret. She didn't want anybody, especially not her parents, to find out."

"That doesn't add up. She told me, she told you, she told her old drama professor. Take it from me, Mike, she wouldn't hide something like this from her parents."

I disagreed. All along, Adrienne had been pathologically worried about her reputation.

"That doesn't mean her family wasn't aware of what was going on," Dave said. "You didn't know her parents. I did, and it would have been perfectly in character for them to learn their daughter was in trouble and recognize somebody had to take care of her. Her father had his job in Washington. Her mother had her political career. They weren't about to drop everything and hold Adrienne's hand for nine months. So you were it, Mike."

Minutes ago I had thought Dave's cynicism was no match for mine. Now I had to rethink. That the Dalys had known I was looking after their daughter in Los Angeles and had been content to have it that way—this was a level of calculation, of cold, bloody-minded Machiavellianism that didn't seem possible. I reminded him that Mrs. Daly had been a puritanical priss, never more so than in her campaign against *The Tropic of Cancer* and *Lady Chatterley's Lover*.

"That was politics," Dave said. "Their personal lives were something else. The Dalys weren't squeamish about sex, and they sure had no illusions about their daughter. They knew I was sleeping with her. One night in bed at my place, she dozed off, and so did I. By the time we woke up, she had missed her curfew. It must have been 3 in the morning, and the sorority housemother had to unlock the front door for us. The way parietal rules worked in those days, the housemother had to notify her parents. Next time I saw her father, he was mad as hell. Not at me, at Adrienne. And not for sleeping with me, but for getting caught. I'll never forget that.

"Another time, when her parents were away, I stayed at the Dalys' house. Adrienne and I were up in her bedroom when her brother walked in and caught us. He might have made a joke or something, but that was all. It was no big deal."

I couldn't believe we were talking about the same person—the girl who hated to have even her obstetrician know she was sexually active.

"Yeah," Dave agreed. "We're both talking about the woman we loved, but it's like a different person. You got the short end of the stick. Bad as it was afterward, I had it good for two years. You got used.

"But you know, Mike, if our positions had been reversed, I'd have done what you did. If you knocked Adrienne up, I'd have happily married her and raised the baby. That's how much I loved her. But I don't have to convince you of that. I guess we're a lot alike."

On this point, I had to dissent. I lacked Dave's good nature and his readiness to forgive. I told him that I had finally felt so provoked by Adrienne that I'd hauled off and smacked her in her pretty face.

He was horrified. "I can't imagine hitting her. It crushed me when she left, but I could never hurt her."

At that, we broke for the evening news. On the enormous flat-screen TV, a correspondent from Rome announced that the conclave of cardinals had elected a new pope. Dave uncorked a bottle of wine and we toasted the pontiff, toasted each other and toasted Amy. Later, a couple of his neighbors joined us, and we went to dinner at a fish restaurant that had a Key West motif, heavy on palm fronds and coconuts. To the accompaniment of Jimmy Buffet on the jukebox, there was more talk about what fools for love Dave and I had been ages ago.

By the time we returned to the house and I was in bed in the guest room, my head spun from fatigue and wine and a full day of talk. But I couldn't sleep, couldn't quit revolving in my mind the notion that part of my past had been ripped inside out like a pocket, spilling loose change and ID cards. I couldn't conceive of how I would ever fumble everything back where it belonged. It wasn't just that I had been off base about Adrienne and Dave. I hardly recognized the person I used to be. In what I had always regarded as "my story," I turned out to be just a ghost along for the ride. This might have been how Amy felt when she found me and believed the last piece of the puzzle had fallen into place—only to discover that her life, like that Escher drawing, consisted of staircases leading to nothing but other staircases.

Next morning Dave confessed that he too had lain awake revising his picture of the past. He maintained that this was doubly hard for him because he had a lousy memory. But he demonstrated sufficient recall to describe a black cocktail dress he had bought Adrienne in 1963. "She was a knockout in it," he said over bacon and eggs. "Do you remember the way her right eye used to slip out of focus when she was tired?"

I told him I did.

"I always liked that," he said.

"A wandering eye," I said. Amblyopia, optometrists call it.

"Yeah, it wandered a hell of a lot more than I realized." But as if he feared that he had been too harsh on Adrienne, he hastened to catalog her good qualities—her sense of humor, intelligence and party skills. I understood his eagerness to accentuate the positive. I too had felt the need to reassure Amy, not to mention myself, that Adrienne wasn't an awful person. Who wants to believe a former lover, much less a mother, is scheming, duplicitous and cold?

For a while Dave and I batted around the idea that Adrienne's problem was that she had been ahead of her time, an independent woman, a protofeminist. For someone with her talent and ambition, it must have been difficult in that era to balance her professional aspirations and her emotional needs. For a successful man, the solution was easy—love the one you're with, enjoy whatever sex is available and arrange your life around your career. But the double standard still deviled women.

Just when we were starting to sound like a two-man consciousness-raising group, a couple of earnest converts to political correctness, Dave puckishly observed, "It does strike me that for an independent woman, Adrienne did always have a knack of landing the right man to help her along. For a while I filled the bill, but I couldn't carry her as high as she meant to go."

"If it makes you feel any better, neither could I."

"No, I think you had a lot of the things she was looking for. You're as smart as her, and she admired artists and writers. If out in California you had written a best-seller and become rich and famous, you'd be with her to this day."

"No. We actually didn't have very much in common. In London, she accused me of bearing a grudge because she wouldn't marry me. But I was more upset by the way she went about things. For an actress, she sure had a terrible sense of timing, and for somebody who became an ambassador, she wasn't much of a diplomat. Look how she dropped you without a backward glance. Look how she brushed off Amy. It wouldn't have cost her much to handle that differently."

"I suppose she could have let us down more gently," he agreed. "But what would that have changed? Adrienne's Adrienne. She did what she had to do." Dave set the scraps of his breakfast on the floor for Killer and poured himself a second cup of coffee. "I don't have any animosity,

Mike. Maybe because, like I told you last night, I do believe I got the better end of the bargain."

A fter I packed for the airport, I spent ten minutes convincing Dave that I should catch a cab. I had already taken up too much of his time. I didn't want him to waste hours driving back and forth. Once he had agreed to that, I tried to persuade him of something far more important. For Amy's sake, as well as his own, they should have a DNA test. I told him I'd pay for it.

Dave promised to consider it but added, "I don't want to do anything that'll hurt Adrienne."

I didn't have an opportunity to say that I didn't see how the truth could hurt anybody. Outside, the taxi honked its horn, and Killer charged the door, barking. Dave and I shook hands, swore we'd keep in touch and have dinner together with our wives one of these days. Then he walked me down the drive and said, "Good-bye, sir."

W riters who quote cab drivers have acquired a deserved reputation for sentimentality or sloppy reporting or fraud or all of the above. But the burly, long-haired headbanger who drove me to Tampa International hollered such pungent wisdom over the thrashing cacophony of a Metallica CD that I can't resist quoting it.

"Who is that guy?" he asked of Dave. "I've seen him around. He looks familiar."

"A fella I knew from college," I said.

"Did he play football? He reminds me of that fullback at Alabama who starred for Bear Bryant."

"You've got the wrong person."

"Then who is he?" the cabbie persisted.

To shut him up, I said, "He's the guy that knocked up my college girlfriend."

This seemed to have the desired effect. He lapsed into silence, and for miles we were serenaded by heavy metal and the hum of tires on the causeway. Then he yelled over his shoulder, "Hey, if you want to talk, I'm all ears."

I figured, Why not? Narrated in these conditions, at high decibel and high speed on the interstate, the tale had a giddy, goofy implausibility perfectly suited to the glare of a Florida afternoon, the blare of Metallica and the beefy disbelief of my driver.

"Jesus," he exclaimed afterward, "that chick's been living rent free in your head forever. Why'd you stay with her?"

"Remember love?" I asked.

"Dimly. Very dimly."

"Well, that's one answer. Of course, there's always a chance I was crazy."

"You said it. Not me. You don't mind my asking, did either you or your buddy marry her?"

"Nope."

"That's one bullet you both dodged."

Had I been quicker on the uptake, and had I had any interest in continuing to trade wisecracks, I might have concurred that Dave and I had survived with minor flesh wounds. Instead, I stared out across the water toward the sawtooth skyline of Tampa, which appeared to be decaying in the heat. The driver broke in to say that a few years back a tugboat had plowed into the bridge we were crossing, knocked loose a number of pilings and concrete slabs and drowned, as he put it, "a mess of people."

I asked him whether he came from Tampa.

"No," he said. "California. Moved east twenty years ago."

"What brought you here?"

Sheepishly ducking his shaggy head, he said, "A girl. I was chasing a girl."

"Did you catch her?" I asked, not unkindly.

"No. She got away, and I got beached here." After a pause, during which the Metallica CD ended and was replaced by Guns n' Roses, he said, "They can make an asshole out of any man, can't they?"

CHAPTER NINETEEN

W eeks later, Dave and Amy agreed to a DNA test. This required submitting a swab from inside their mouths. With Amy living on the West Coast and Dave on the East Coast, the logistics were complicated. He had to drive to an office some distance from his home, and Amy had to juggle her schedule to rendezvous with a lab technician at her house. Then both samples had to be dispatched to the Midwest for analysis.

But neither of them complained of the inconvenience, nor did they dwell on the possible consequences—disappointment for Dave, another dead end for Amy. Judging by Adrienne's attitude to date, she wasn't apt to clear up matters in the event of a negative result, and I couldn't imagine where Amy would turn next in the search for her biological father. The "third man" was the most plausible candidate, but if he was still alive, he had to be in his eighties by now, and while I knew his name, I had qualms about my chances of tracing him.

For a novelist, yet another twist in the plot, a dramatic last-minute reversal, always has its appeal. At some level, it tantalized me to think that a final revelation might tie up all the loose ends. But in a different, sunnier corner of my soul, having met and liked Dave, I hoped there would be good news for him.

The day of the DNA results, Dave let me listen in on a conference call with the lab. A woman informed him that he had to verify his identity with his birth date and driver's-license number.

"My wallet's out in the car," he said. "Lemme get it."

He plunked down the phone, and Killer barked, then began panting into the receiver. The woman at the lab chuckled. "Usually they're carrying a cell phone, and you hear the door slam and the glove compartment open and shut. I think I'd rather listen to all that banging around than this heavy breathing."

When Dave returned and recited his license number, the woman said, "I'll read the result now. Then I'll explain what it means. Afterward you can ask questions." She cleared her throat. "The test indicates that Dave cannot be excluded as the father. This means you are the father."

"I knew it," Dave exclaimed. "I never had any doubt."

"Do you have questions?" she asked.

Dave didn't. But I inquired about the statistical accuracy of the test.

"Ninety-nine percent," she said.

"I knew it," Dave repeated, exuberant. "How do you feel, Mike?"

I admitted I felt relieved.

As for how Amy felt, I would have to wait to find out. A magazine assignment took me to Madrid, and after a week's drive through Spain and France with Linda, I covered the French Open tennis tournament in Paris. Dave was in town with his wife, Paulette, so we had that promised dinner *en famille* much sooner than anticipated. The four of us agreed it was a shame Amy wasn't there to join the celebration.

As we lingered in the Latin Quarter over liqueurs, Linda said, "I wonder what Adrienne would think if she knew you two had gotten together to compare notes."

Paulette laughed and said, "It serves the conniving bitch right."

"Hey, no," Dave protested. "She was never a bitch."

There was a kind of grandeur, a nobility, to his refusal to accept or express any criticism of Adrienne. Dave's protective instinct toward his old flame had hardened into shimmering amber. For him, she would always remain the beautiful girl in the black cocktail dress, the one with the wandering eye and the voice full of money. That he had lost her must have seemed to him a mystery every bit as unfathomable as the fact that he had had her in the first place.

And what, I wondered, did Adrienne remain for me? A dodged bullet, as the cabbie in Tampa put it? One of those vivid characters, encountered more often in novels than in real life, whose influence, both bad and good, ends up educating a young man? Yes, one way or another, she had taught me a lot. So much of who I am and what I am was forged by that brief, incandescent exposure to Adrienne Daly. While, unlike Dave, I now had a gimlet-eyed view of her, I wasn't deluded that hard-won knowledge was all I had limped away with. Whatever her intentions, she had opened a wider world for me, and even in her absence I had found my place in it. After many missteps, I had left behind that college boy on the roadside with his books wrapped in newspapers and had become the man, the husband, the father I am today.

What mattered for more than this, however, was that Amy had been born. That I had had some role in this pleased me. While I regretted that I had missed watching her grow up, I'm not convinced that her life would have been bettered by my presence. Given the ugliness of my breakup with Adrienne, I hate to imagine the bloody disaster a divorce might have been. Even if Adrienne and I had managed to stay together,

I don't believe Amy would have become the happy woman she is today. Not with me as her father—brooding, restless, rootless, alternately angry and depressed. Far better for her to have enjoyed the genetic leavening of her lighthearted birth father and the kind, loving care of her adoptive mother. The best I had to offer her was given before she was born.

This wasn't to say that I didn't crave ongoing contact. In fact, I found myself indulging in a fantasy every bit as literary and unrealistic as Dave's Gatsbyesque daydreams about Adrienne. When I learned that Amy and her husband and their three children intended to pass through London on their way to a vacation in France, I began to plan a meeting between the two families. Having moved from the flat in Hampstead to a house in St. John's Wood, I pictured the kids playing in our garden while the grownups drank Pimm's on the terrace. Then, as in the last chapter of a nineteenth-century novel, there would be a scene of resolution and reconciliation as we all sat down to dinner together.

But it didn't work out that way. After an eleven-hour flight from Los Angeles, Amy and her family arrived in London exhausted and frazzled. Amy hadn't lost her sense of humor, though. She joked that her two-year-old son had "baptized" Virgin Atlantic's upper-class sleeper suite, vomiting as the plane landed. The whole crew of them, which included a nanny, headed straight to their hotel, the Four Seasons on Hyde Park. Amy apologized but said that they were in no shape for dinner at my place.

Since they were leaving the next day, I suggested we reschedule the meal for Paris. It was no trouble for Linda and me to catch the Eurostar to France. That suited Amy, who told me they'd be at the George V. Linda and I could stop by to meet the kids, then the four adults could eat dinner out while the nanny babysat.

Belatedly, it sank in why Amy had stressed from the start that Adrienne needn't worry that she was angling for a handout. Six tickets on

Virgin upper class. Suites at The Four Seasons and the George V. From Paris, they planned to fly to the Riviera. It delighted me that she had landed on her feet and in clover. Born to a rich couple, brought up modestly, she was, in fairy-tale fashion, now wealthy.

I made restaurant reservations for 8:30 P.M., and Linda and I showed up at the George V an hour and a half early to spend time with Amy's family. We must have appeared to be frustrated grandparents, impatient with our bachelor sons. I hadn't gauged how our eagerness might seem from Amy's perspective. How was she supposed to explain these strangers to her kids? Maybe that was why she chose to join us in the lobby and deal with the introductions at the concierge's desk. Then the kids were handed off to the Latin American nanny, and after Linda had snapped a few photographs, we were out in front with a liveried bell captain escorting us to a cab.

With time to kill, we stopped for drinks at Café Marly, overlooking the glass pyramid that glinted in evening sunlight in the courtyard of the Louvre. Amy wore a black cocktail dress that would likely have reminded Dave of the one he had bought Adrienne. Cut low in the back, it showed off the tan contours of her shoulders and the smooth, notched column of her spine.

Jason, who bore an uncanny resemblance to the actor Benicio del Toro, had a pair of mirrored sunglasses tucked into his unbuttoned collar. His shirt hung loose at the waist; an even looser jacket was draped from his thick shoulders. He wore black loafers without socks. Since one of his businesses had been movie lighting, he and Linda discussed films while I attempted to coax from Amy her reaction to the DNA test.

It wouldn't be quite accurate to say she was evasive. And it would be unfair to observe that she sounded indifferent to the news that Dave was definitely her father. But the subject didn't seem to engage her full attention. Ordering a martini straight up, she said, as she had many times, "I wasn't looking for a father. Or a mother, for that matter. I had parents. I just wanted information. Now that I've had kids and they're healthy, the rest of it doesn't seem so important."

For a while the four of us talked about their trip to the Riviera. They had booked at a resort a dozen miles inland from Nice, near the walled town of Tourettes-sur-Loup. Linda and I had lived in the area for years. We knew its every obscure bend and elbow—restaurants to recommend, tourist traps to avoid, playgrounds the kids would love, out-of-the-way beaches where the water was clean. When Jason mentioned that they planned to spend one night in St. Tropez and another in Monte Carlo, it was on the tip of my tongue to tell him, No, don't do that. Fortunately, I held back. I would have sounded like an intrusive father. Worse, a grandfather.

From the Louvre, we strolled to the Palais Royal, stopping for photo ops en route, then crossing an expanse of dusty white pebbles between *allées* of chestnut trees that some topiary artist had trimmed into precise rectangles. At a restaurant in the far corner of the arcade, we sat at a table outdoors. As night fell and the temperature dipped a precious few degrees, I struggled not to make a fool of myself and proclaim how much it delighted me to be here in a city I loved, with people I loved. Already I had an uneasy sense that this meant far more to me than to them.

After a glass of wine, Amy cut short the polite gabble about the glories of French cuisine and asked, "Would you still be interested in me if I was fat and lived in a trailer with three kids by three different men?"

Could there have been a more pointed admonition that I didn't know her nearly as well as I believed I did? Had I been in danger of making the same mistake as with her birth mother—trying to make her into the woman I had imagined? I told her I was familiar with trailers, single mothers and absent fathers. I had grown up in that world. But wherever Amy lived, however she looked, I would want to know her.

"That would make it a different story, though, wouldn't it?" she said.

"So would a lot of other things. Your mother told me there was a baby girl she could have adopted two years before you were born. She might have taken that one, and you'd have been raised by somebody else. What the hell, you might have been raised by me.

"Here we are discussing things that might have been different," I switched tacks, "but when I was with Dave, he told me something that would have been the same. He said if I had gotten Adrienne pregnant, he would have done what I did—stay with her, offer to marry her and keep you."

Amy said, "I can believe that."

"I can't," Jason said.

"What if one of your boys were in that situation?" I asked her. "What would you advise him?"

"It would depend on how much he loved the girl."

"I can't believe this," Jason said.

"Well, if he loved her," Amy said, "I wouldn't necessarily encourage him to marry her. Not at twenty or twenty-one. But I hope he'd help her."

"I can't believe this," Jason repeated.

"I assume you agree with me," I said. "You'd tell your son to steer clear."

"Sure," Jason said. "But what I can't believe is why you're holding on to this after forty years."

The table went silent. The rush of blood in my ears went up in volume.

"I guess you look at things as a writer." he said. "I'm a businessman. When it's over, you move on."

I sipped my wine. I glanced at Amy. I looked at Linda. I might have mentioned that I had moved on for more than thirty years before Amy had phoned my sister. I might have maintained that the story had pursued me, not vice versa. I might have quoted the Greek adage that stories happen to those who can tell them. I might have pointed out that there was something emblematically American about a tale that was now as much Jason's as it was mine. Part Hispanic, part Apache, he had been raised on an Indian reservation, made himself into a millionaire and married a beautiful adopted girl brought up by a single mother in straitened circumstances. Now he discovered that . . .

I decided not to bother. Instead, I told Jason, "I see what you're saying."

The four of us finished our meal. The food was excellent—risotto, crab salad, foie gras, sea bass and two bottles of wine from the chef's vineyard outside Carcasonne. We ordered a single dessert, a chocolate fondant, and shared it with four spoons, daintily dabbing up the last rich crumbs from the plate. They were good company, Amy and Jason. I could envision an evening with them in Los Angeles, where Jason promised us the best Mexican food we'd ever taste. I could envision us becoming . . . no, not family, but friends.

After dinner, as we crossed Avenue de l'Opéra toward a cab stand, they invited us back to the George V for a drink. They weren't ready to call it a night. But for me, the evening was fine as it was. The tricky thing about children is knowing how long to hold on to them. Whether you're a birth father, an adoptive mother or a surrogate parent, in the end you have to realize when to let go. Linda and I gave them hugs and kisses and watched the taxi take them away.